Growing Up is Hard to Do

REFLECTIONS ON YOUR EARLIEST BEGINNINGS
TO YOUR LATE TEENAGE YEARS

JAY SPENCE, MD

◆ FriesenPress

Suite 300 - 990 Fort St
Victoria, BC, V8V 3K2
Canada

www.friesenpress.com

Copyright © 2017 by Dr. Jay Spence, MD, FRCS(C)
First Edition — 2017

Illustratated by Ian Baker

All rights reserved.

No part of this publication may be reproduced in any form, or by any means, electronic or mechanical, including photocopying, recording, or any information browsing, storage, or retrieval system, without permission in writing from FriesenPress.

ISBN
978-1-5255-1177-6 (Hardcover)
978-1-5255-1178-3 (Paperback)
978-1-5255-1179-0 (eBook)

1. JUVENILE NONFICTION, HEALTH & DAILY LIVING, MATURING
2. YOUNG ADULT NONFICTION, SOCIAL TOPICS, DRUGS, ALCOHOL, SUBSTANCE ABUSE
3. YOUNG ADULT NONFICTION, BODY, MIND & SPIRIT

Distributed to the trade by The Ingram Book Company

Dedicated to our grandchildren

Adelaide

Benjamin

Kai

Alexandra

Asher

Claire

Table of Contents

INTRODUCTION — x

GROWING UP — 1

CHAPTER ONE: THE BEGINNINGS: INTRAUTERINE LIFE — 3

"Where Did I Come From?"

Genetics	"Nature's Blueprint For Me."	6
Intrauterine Growth	"In My Mummy's Tummy."	12
Labour and Delivery	"Here I Come!"	20

CHAPTER TWO: EARLY CHILDHOOD — 23

Newborn to Age Five

Infancy: Newborn to Age One	"It's All About Me!"	25
Toddler: Age One to Two	"Becoming Me."	28
The Terrible Twos!	"Here I Am!"	30
Energizer Bunny: Age Three to Four	"Want to Play With Me?"	31
Youngster: Age Four to Five	"Out on My Own."	34

CHAPTER THREE: SCHOOL AGE: AGE FIVE TO TEN   37

"I'm off to school!"

School . . . . "I Don't Want to Go!"	39
My Social Life . . . . "I Like You."	41
Bullies . . . . "Get Out of My Way!"	42
Childhood Responsibilities . . . . "Who, Me—Work?"	43

CHAPTER FOUR: PUBERTY: AGE TEN TO FIFTEEN   45

"Wow! What's Happening to Me?"

Physical Changes	48
Female Development	52
Male Development	60

CHAPTER FIVE: ADOLESCENCE: AGE TWELVE TO EIGHTEEN   63

"I feel different!"

Sexual, Emotional, and Intellectual Development	65
Early Adolescence	66
Late Adolescence	67

THE HARD-TO-DO 71

CHAPTER SIX: SEX 73
    Sexual Identity 76
        Female 82
        Male 84
    The Birds and the Bees 88

CHAPTER SEVEN: SEXUAL ISSUES 91
    Early Human Sexuality 93
    Sexual Abuse 94
    Pornography and Children 95
    Sexting 96
    Early Sexual Experimentation 97

CHAPTER EIGHT: THE CANDY GENERATION 99
    Cultural Challenges 101
    Sex Drive 103
        Male 103
        Female 104

CHAPTER NINE: UNWANTED PREGNANCY 107
    Startling facts 109
    Teenage Mom 110
    Teenage Abortion 112

CHAPTER TEN: ALTERNATE SEXUAL BEHAVIOURS — 115
    Homosexuality — 117
    LGBTQ Community — 120
    Of Real Concern — 121
        Abusive Sex — 121
        Teenage Prostitution — 122

CHAPTER ELEVEN: SEXUALLY TRANSMITTED DISEASES — 125
    Genital Herpes — 128
    Human Papilloma Virus (HPV) — 129
    Chlamydia — 130
    Trichomonas (TRICH) — 131
    Gonorrhea — 132
    Syphilis — 133
    HIV-AIDS — 134

CHAPTER TWELVE: RISKY BEHAVIOUR — 135
    Smoking — 138
    Alcohol — 140
    Marijuana — 143

CHAPTER THIRTEEN: DESTRUCTIVE BEHAVIOUR — 145

    Illegal Drug Use — 147

        Cocaine — 149

        Opioids — 150

        Stimulants — 151

        Ecstasy — 152

        Hallucinogens — 153

        Inhalants — 154

    Suicide Attempts — 155

CHAPTER FOURTEEN: LIFESTYLE CHOICES — 157

    Diet and Nutrition — 159

        Teenage Obesity — 160

        Anorexia — 162

        Bulimia — 163

    Exercise — 164

CHAPTER FIFTEEN: INTERNET AND THE TEENAGE DRIVER — 165

    The Internet, Social Media, and Gaming — 167

    Wheels: Risks and Concerns — 170

        Some Startling Facts — 172

        Risk factors — 173

CHAPTER SIXTEEN: BECOMING AN ADULT 175

Eighteen-Plus

Higher Education 178

FINAL THOUGHTS 180

ACKNOWLEDGEMENTS 182

ABOUT THE AUTHOR 185

ABOUT THE ILLUSTRATOR 186

Introduction

Introduction

Why me? Who am I? The most important, yet challenging problem for your life will be to have some insight about your very being—ultimately, who you are. This is not an easy question at the best of times, but especially when you are young. Even with family and friends nearby, we often feel alone, not only with our thoughts, but also as we try to figure out everything that is happening around us. This book is meant to give you, as a young person, basic, helpful information and to provide some guidance as you go through the early stages of your life.

Before getting started, I must explain why I feel I have the right to comment on another person's life—your life—and the issues you will face and need to understand. Simply put, I wish I had had a guide or a mentor at each stage of my life. Sadly, I was on my own, making most of my life's decisions with little or no information to guide me. I made many mistakes; some I regret to this day. I was lucky to get by, obtain an education, survive, and, over time, negotiate many of life's perils.

Introduction

Months ago, as I was sitting at my desk with pictures of my wife, our children, and our grandchildren staring out at me, I began to reflect on life in general and on young people's challenges in particular. How best could I share my life's ups, downs, and other experiences, learned the hard way, especially with our grandchildren, who are just starting out on their life journeys? Yes, life is full of many issues (joys, sadness, disappointments, losses, loves, hurts, injuries, and many other "hills to climb") which we all have to face at one time or another.

When I think back, I realize that each of us has to function in many roles over time. Each role gives us new perspectives and many lessons in what works and what doesn't. In my case, I was born a male, grew up through adolescence, and became an adult. I was a son to my parents, a brother to my three siblings, was and remain a husband, and am now a father of three (two daughters and a son), each of whom has two children with their partners—so that today I am also a father-in-law, and a grandfather to six.

In my professional life, nearly fifty years ago I became a medical doctor. I have been listening to, learning about, and caring for thousands of patients over the years, specializing with a specific interest in young females and their adolescent problems. I became a teacher, a professor at a university, and the head of a department with hospital administrative duties. Now retired, in my early seventies, I serve on a few volunteer charity boards and try to give back to the financially disadvantaged.

Introduction

From these many vantage points, which I have shared with others over a lifetime, I have witnessed a great deal. As well, my wife and I have had the privilege of living and travelling in many countries, observing different societies and cultures. I wish to impart what I have experienced and learned throughout my life in the hope that it will be of interest and possibly helpful to our own grandchildren and other young people who might also be encouraged to think more deeply about their own individual lives.

Today life is more complicated than when I grew up. No real guidelines are easily available to understand and negotiate this complex world. Because our society and many others have looser social structures these days, your life may be difficult—even treacherous—and have many undesirable consequences. In the following pages I will try to provide an overview and make comments on each stage of your early life. I will attempt to identify "the potholes" in as simple and plain language as possible, so that everyone can understand the troubling issues that may be encountered along the way. Your parents or others may want to take part and use what I have written to set the stage for more in-depth discussions. That might be a good thing, but this is your book, so let's get started—at the beginning.

GROWING UP

Chapter One

THE BEGINNINGS: INTRAUTERINE LIFE

"Where Did I Come From?"

The Beginnings: Intrauterine Life

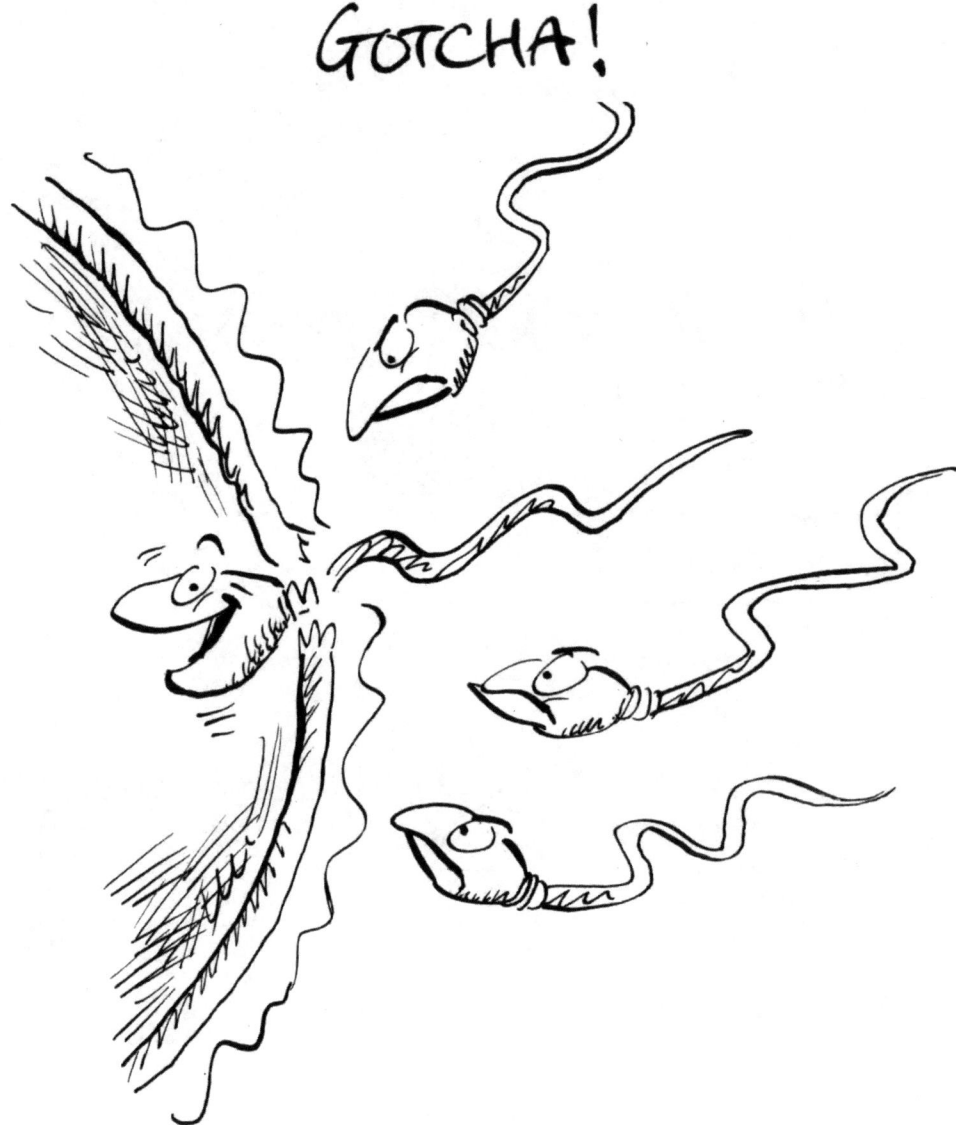

GENETICS

"Nature's Blueprint For Me."

One thing is certain: we can't choose our parents. Genetically, we are what we are. The term "human genetics" refers to the directions for building a human being like you. The directions are written in code form, but they are very specific and are found in the first cell, or building block, that you arose from. That first cell was formed when an egg of your mother's was united with, or fertilized by, a sperm from your father. (More on that later.) So, half the building directions originally came from your mother and half from your father. You are unique—one of a kind. Your brothers or sisters can be similar, but since each egg and each sperm are like no other, with different building instructions in them, none of us can ever be the same, unless you have an identical twin. In that case, the initial fertilized cell split in two, giving rise to two separate, matching cells that each went on to develop.

The Beginnings: Intrauterine Life

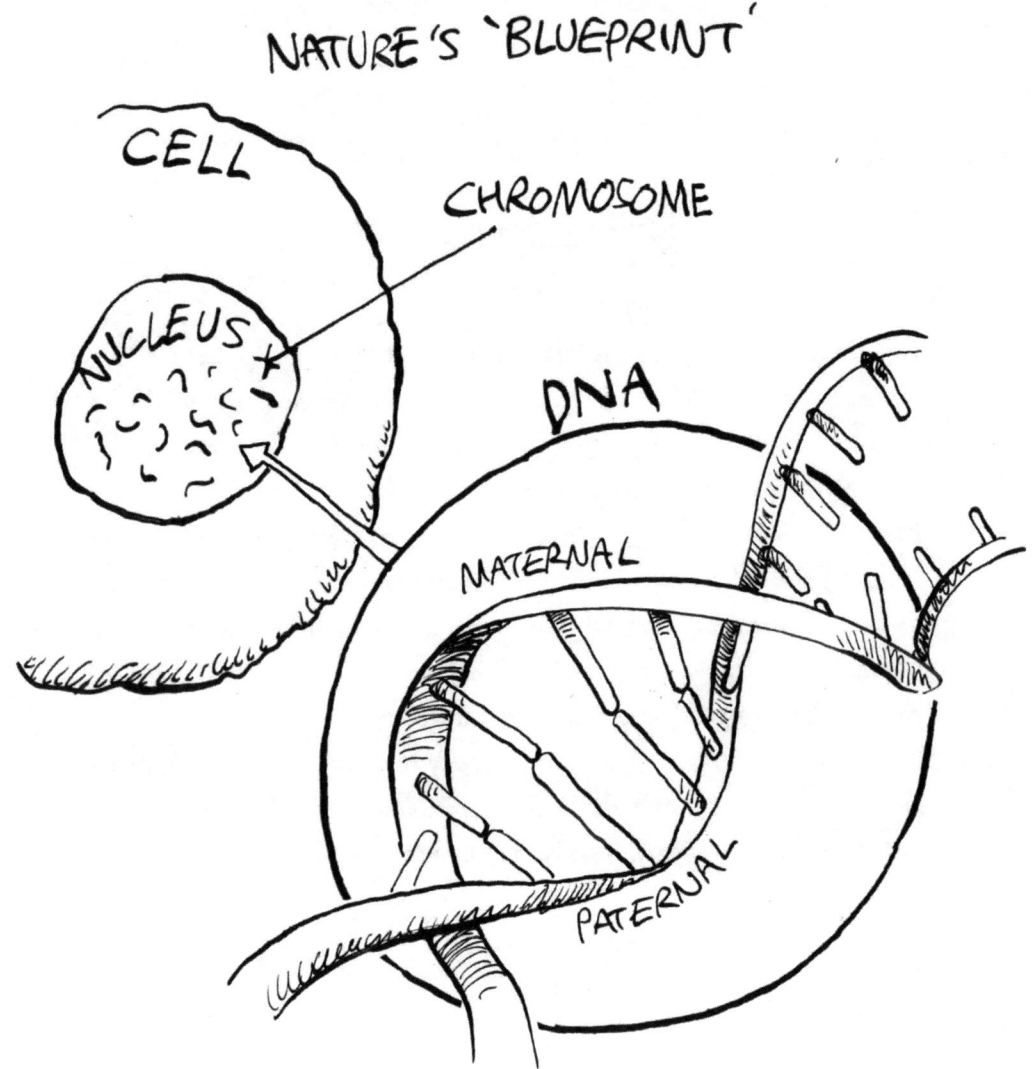

The genetic information that makes up the directions for your growth is similar to a plan to build a Lego toy or to blueprints for building a house. These directions are stored in all the cells that will make up your body, in a special, central position in each cell called the nucleus. Inside the nucleus are the chromosomes, which are the genetic threads on which the information is stored. For simplicity, the individual chromosomes look like X's. Think of the right half of the X as from one parent and the left half of the X as from the other parent.

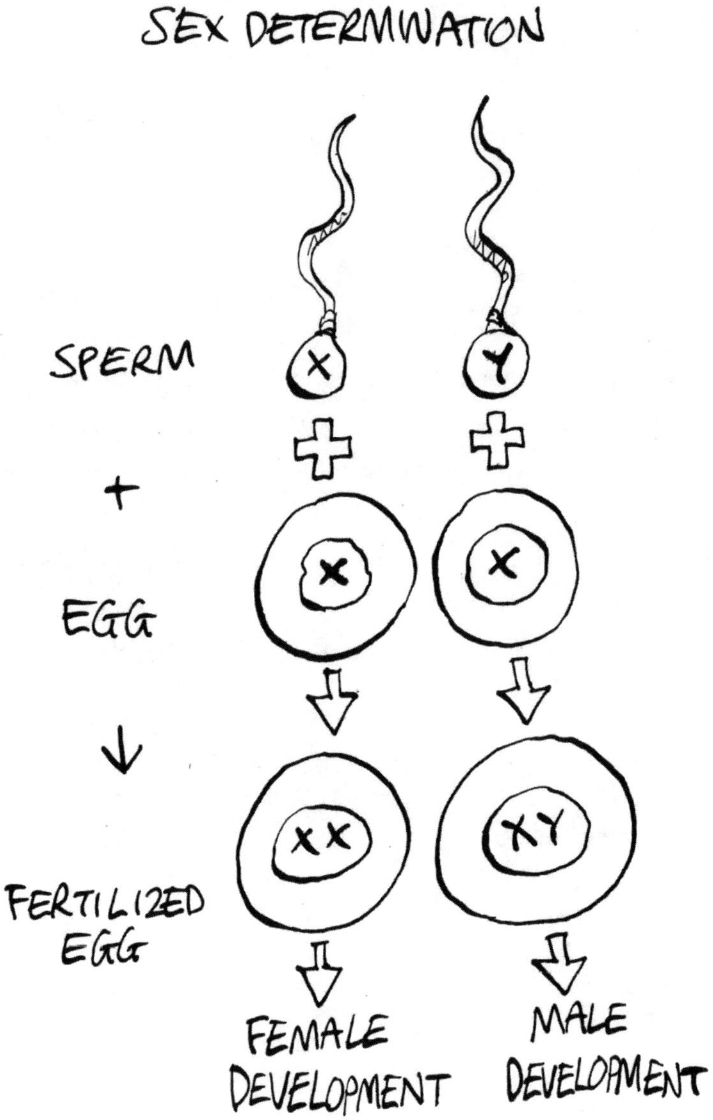

The Beginnings: Intrauterine Life

SEX DETERMINATION

SPERM

\+

EGG

↓

FERTILIZED EGG

FEMALE DEVELOPMENT

MALE DEVELOPMENT

Humans have forty-six (46) chromosomes. The chromosomes themselves are made up of thousands of genes; again, half from each parent. Similar genes then become pairs, so that we think of humans having twenty-three (23) pairs of chromosomes. Twenty-two (22) of these determine most of our inherited features. One pair, (number 23) is made of two sex chromosomes that determine the sex we will become. If the first cell contains the sex chromosome X from your mother (xx) and an X from your father (xy), then you will become a female (xx). If, however, the sperm provides a Y, then you will develop into a male (xy). All the other chromosomes, (which happen to look like a twisted ladder) are made up of multiple genes, and direct every other aspect of your physical self—maybe even how you will eventually think and be able to perform.

The Beginnings: Intrauterine Life

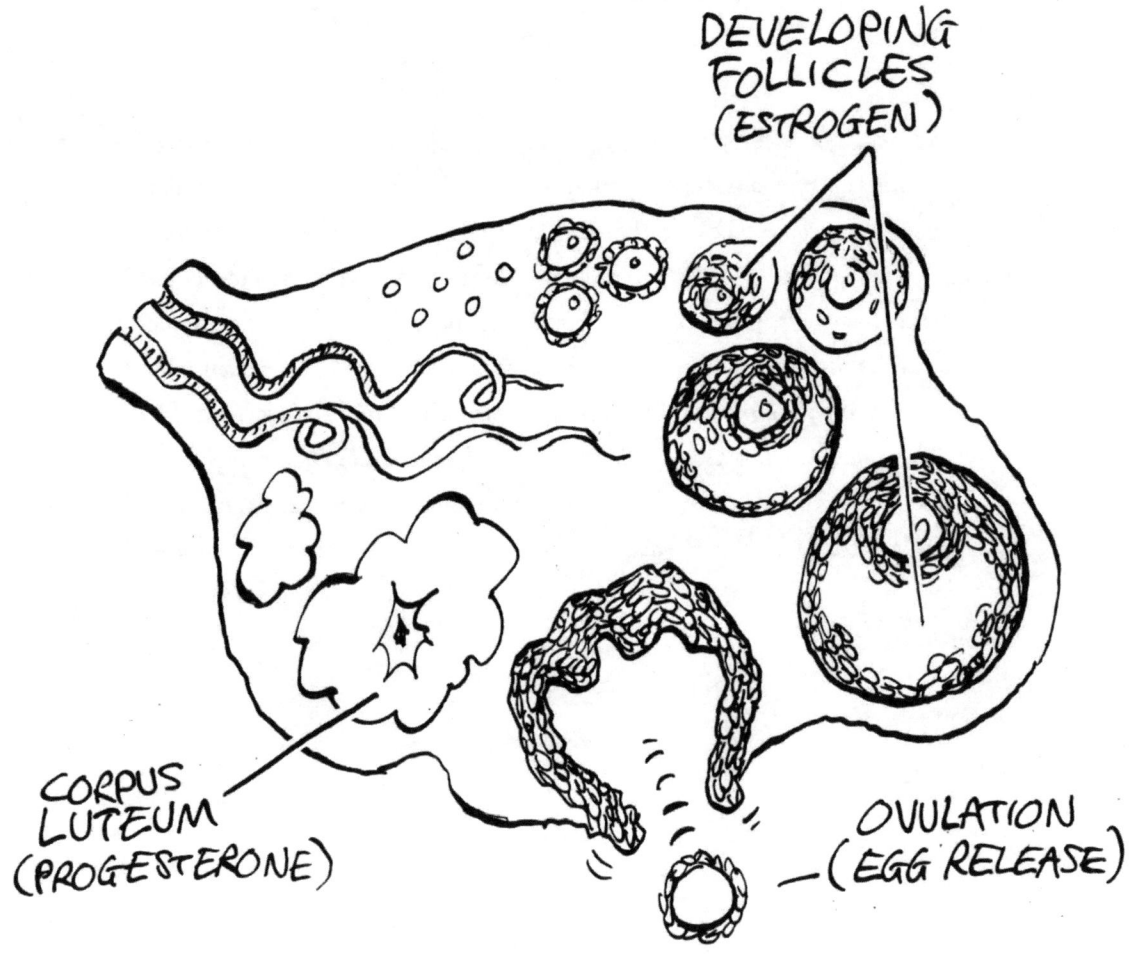

INTRAUTERINE GROWTH

"In My Mummy's Tummy."

First, an egg is released from one of the mother's ovaries, which store all her eggs. The egg is picked up from the ovary by a fallopian tube, which is connected to the uterus. Many of the father's sperm make their way to this tube and are attracted to the egg.

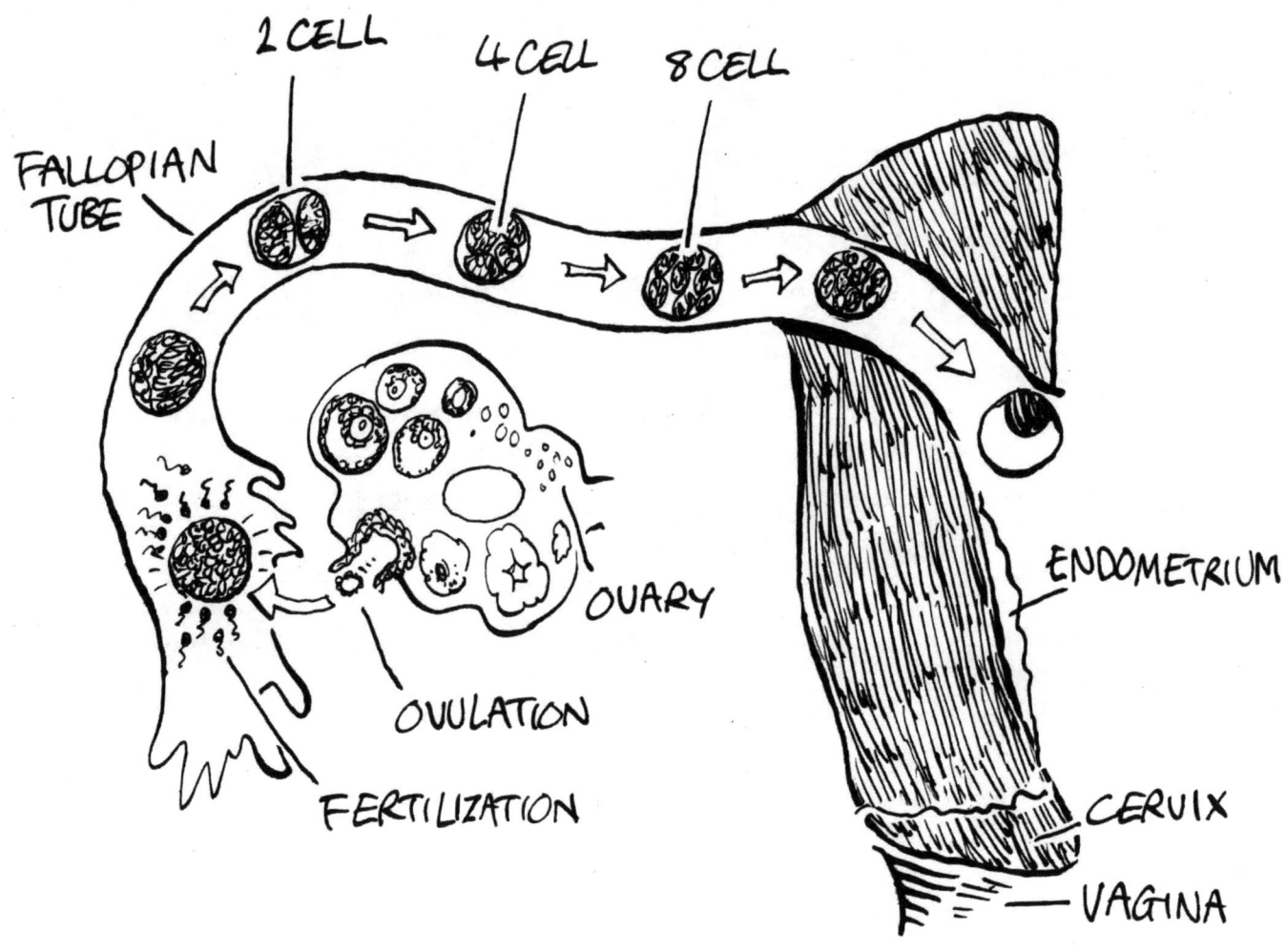

Intrauterine Growth

When the egg and sperm unite, the process is called fertilization. The fertilized cell then moves along the fallopian tube, entering into the mother's growth chamber; her uterus.

The Beginnings: Intrauterine Life

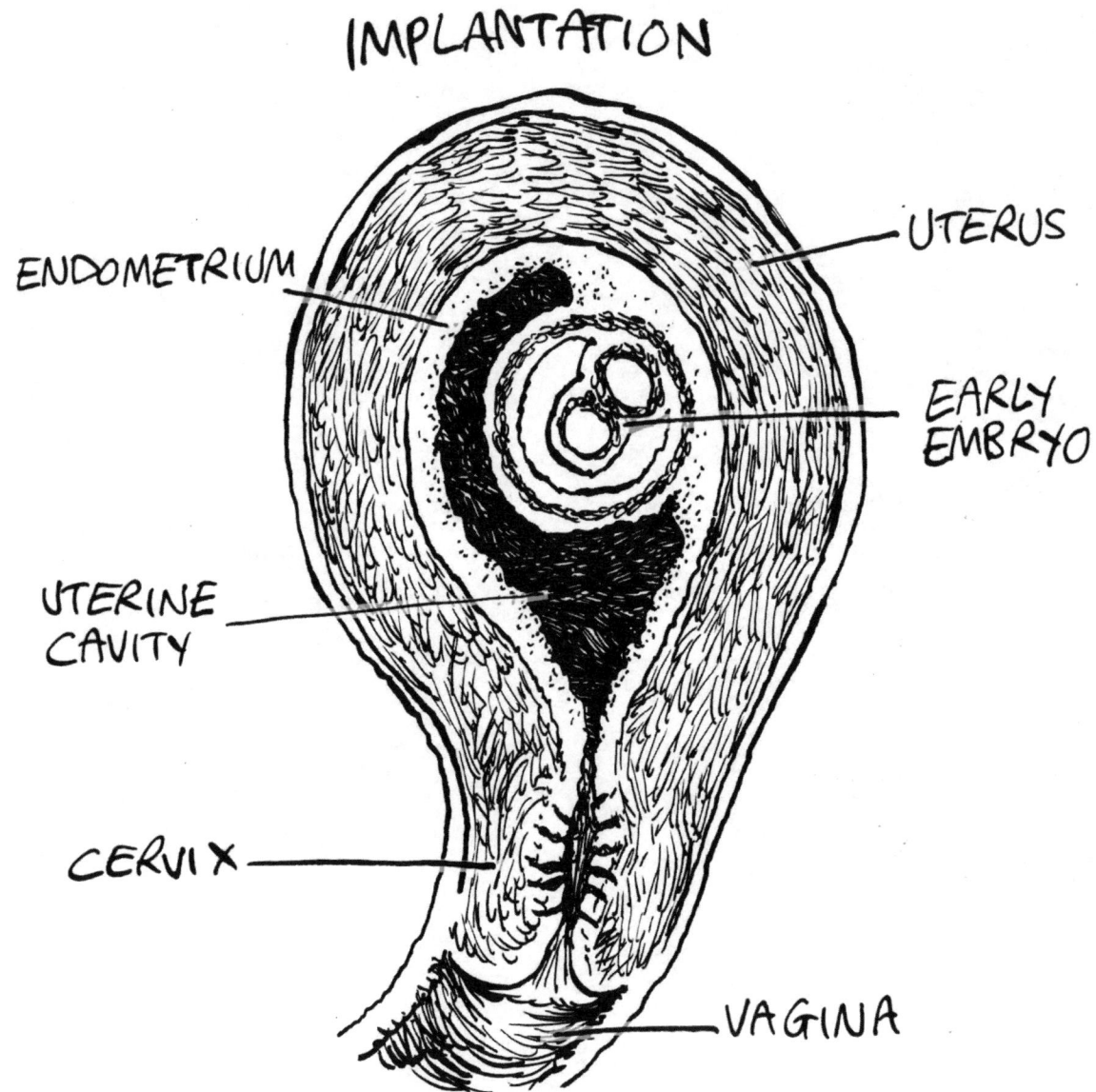

That one cell begins to divide rapidly under the proper conditions and implants itself into the lining (endometrium) of the uterus. (Think of this lining as like the soil that plants grow in.) The uterus is located in the mother's lower abdomen, called the pelvis.

There, the early ball of cells (the embryo) is well protected. To accommodate this growing life, the uterus also expands until it almost fills the mother's abdomen (or belly, as you might think of it).

The Beginnings: Intrauterine Life

MID PREGNANCY

- UTERUS
- PLACENTA
- UMBILICAL CORD
- DEVELOPING FETUS
- UTERINE CAVITY
- CERVIX
- VAGINA

The initial cell first divides into two, then four, then eight, then sixteen, and on and on. Over time, some of these cells start to divide at different rates from the rest, forming a more humanlike body, with head, limbs, and internal organs such as heart, lungs, and kidneys becoming easily identifiable. Initially, the cells of the embryo further divide and transform into the earliest form of the baby (fetus), which after nine months of growth will have matured completely into a full-term baby. All this time, the fetus has been protected and fed by the mother through the umbilical cord. This umbilical cord connects the mother to the baby.

The Beginnings: Intrauterine Life

LABOUR AND DELIVERY
"Here I Come!"

Through the umbilical cord and its blood circulation, the fetus (or unborn child) communicates to the mother that its growth in the uterus is complete. The mother's reproductive system, in some circumstances, can also initiate labour. Though the uterus has been expanding to accommodate the fetus for nine months, now it begins to noticeably tighten and contract, growing smaller. At first the contractions are irregular and painless, but then they become more regular and increasingly painful. After what are usually hours of contractions (the process of labour), the infant is expelled from the uterus through a passageway called the vagina, and into the outside world. This whole process can sometimes be long and drawn out. If problems occur during the pregnancy or delivery, the baby may have to be delivered by surgery through the mother's abdomen. This procedure is called a caesarean section.

The Beginnings: Intrauterine Life

Once delivered, you, as an infant, take your first breath, and begin to cry and look around at a strange new world. You are no longer in a dark, warm, protected place, but out in the cold, with lights all around and sounds galore. Just after your birth, the most important decision about your life, your gender, is made, usually by a complete stranger—the person who helped deliver you. That caregiver informs your mother and your father, if he is present, that you're a boy or a girl, and the course of your life is decided. The umbilical cord is cut and your belly button is all that remains of that physical attachment you once had to your mother.

Labour and Delivery

Now you can see why Mother's Day is one of those special times celebrated each year, when we recognize where we came from, the nourishment we received, and the support that was necessary for our lives to begin!

Your mother, by giving birth to you, will unconditionally love you for as long as she and you live. That love, over time, grows and will provide you with comfort and support in the many years ahead. Fathers, too, are critical to your growth and development. However, it often takes more time for your father to build that special relationship with you.

Chapter Two

EARLY CHILDHOOD

Newborn to Age Five

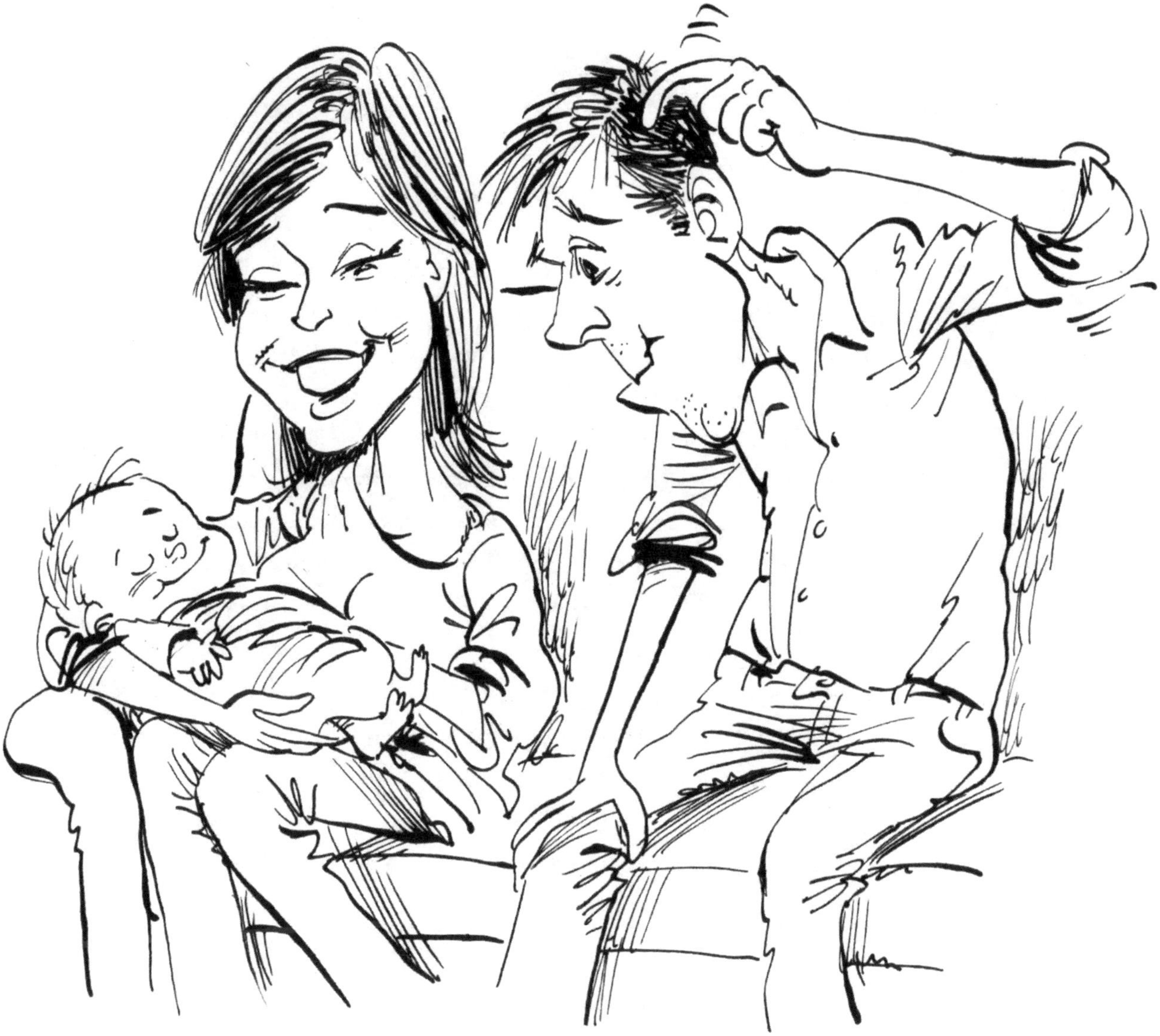

INFANCY: NEWBORN TO AGE ONE
"It's All About Me!"

What a change! You have been growing for nine months in complete darkness, bathed in the amniotic fluid in your mother's uterus, supplied constantly with nourishment in a warm and protected environment and with only muffled sounds to please your ears. Suddenly you are thrust into a strange new world, full of bright lights, in a cooler and possibly drafty place with no food and all the while just trying to breathe. You are no longer attached to a food source and are being constantly touched, passed about, and looked at. Overwhelming! No wonder the first few days of your life are stressful. Your mother relates to you but doesn't really know you. You may be her first child, so she has to learn how to care for you. Even if she has had other children, you are completely different, with your own personal needs and preferences.

Humans, at the top of the animal kingdom, are unique in that their young cannot survive without their mothers or the wider family's care. We cannot feed ourselves, nor can we move, or even keep ourselves warm. Each of us, as newborns and infants, is totally dependent on others to live, grow, and fully develop.

Infancy: Newborn to Age One

The first few weeks and months of life are all about getting bodily functions working. At first, just breathing is critical to survival, but next is learning to feed. A mother's breast milk is the best source of nourishment, but sometimes it is not easy for the mother to relax and embrace this new experience. It may also be hard for the infant to latch on to the breasts. Some stress and anxiety can result from these problems, in both the mother and child, which, if not corrected, can lead to inadequate nourishment for the newborn infant. These problems should and can be corrected with knowledgeable support. Some mothers prefer to feed their offspring formula, which is perfectly satisfactory. Cultural practices, educational levels, and other concerns play a role in deciding what nutrition a child receives. In addition, sleep schedules have to be worked out to meet the child's needs and desires. Crying is normal and doesn't necessarily mean there's anything wrong – it can be just a way to ventilate! The mother and father quickly learn about their child's needs, their rhythms, and how to provide personal comfort.

Early Childhood

After about three months of life, babies begin to discover more about their bodies. They can initiate purposeful movements of their limbs and hands. They will raise their heads. Soon, young infants begin to use their hands more and can roll from stomach to back. In the next months, they can weight-bear when held. By eight months, infants will usually start to crawl, may sit, and by one year, can stand if holding onto something. Shortly thereafter, children take their first steps and are soon cruising around the house. There can be great variation from child to child in reaching these milestones that, nevertheless, usually falls into the "normal" range.

During the second half of the first year, infants start making sounds and may say a few basic words a few months later. By the time they reach their first birthday, they certainly understand the word "NO!" Also during this time frame, children can eat finger foods and soft food from a spoon. They begin to put everything in their mouths as well, so parents have to be careful. By the end of year one, they have been smiling and socializing for a while and more interaction with others begins.

TODDLER: AGE ONE TO TWO
"Becoming Me."

After the first year of life, the infant stage is gone. Now you are not so dependent on your parents. You are no longer a helpless baby doll! You can get around, show your preferences for what you eat, what you want to play with and when you want to go to sleep. You are beginning the process of individualization. You're becoming your own person.

During these early years a child is totally dependent on the family for all the necessities of life: food, protection, warmth, and emotional support. Yet a young child will begin to push back, and often the parents can feel rejected. This is normal and it is how children grow to be independent human beings. A new relationship is developing.

Socially, the child begins to explore, yet wants to be reassured that Mommy and Daddy are nearby. Strangers are to be studied, but from a distance. Parents should foster this independence, although within an environment of security. Children want, and need to explore their environments. They are and should be curious, putting themselves in situations that may cause them some harm. Naturally, parents want to protect their children from injury, but small mishaps should be permitted and even welcomed, as this is how we all learn. We learn best when there are unintended consequences, even if it means getting hurt a bit. Children often learn the hard way: "That was not such a great idea!" Life teaches us all, especially early on. The important thing for all children is that they have some freedom in supervised play, and are able to try out new things. It is also of great benefit to be around other children and other adults in various situations. Children need and want to feel secure, but without rigid restraints.

Early Childhood

THE TERRIBLE TWOS!
"Here I Am!"

Around two years of age, children begin to come into their own. They have full mobility and are developing language skills and beginning to enjoy some independence. Sadly, this new boldness is not entirely justified as they are still mostly dependent, requiring a loving relationship but becoming increasingly selfish. "NO!" becomes the operative word, when "Yes" is the answer parents are looking for.

Young children learn best by example. They want to copy what others around them are doing. Through imitation the child learns a great deal, so it is important for the family to always be on their best behaviour. "Please" and "Thank you" from parents foster the same polite responses in their children. Nastiness, negativity, poor language, and violence have no place in the education of children. Sadly, the child can be a bystander and have no choice in the matter. Too often, inappropriate behaviour, swearing, and— most concerning—physical conflict leave a troubling imprint on the youngster exposed to them.

Imagination, which is critical to growth, comes through play. Whether it is with the simplest of toys, such as pots and pans, shoes or water, or more sophisticated and often costly toys, these activities are the way children express themselves. Being outside in the fresh air gives them endless things to do, whether in a park, playground, sandbox, or the woods. Picture books, blocks, paper, and crayons keep children engaged for hours indoors. Make-believe is magical and should be part of all our lives.

ENERGIZER BUNNY: AGE THREE TO FOUR
"Want to Play With Me?"

Toddlers just want to be active. It's all about burning off an enormous amount of built up energy. Developmentally, these youngsters are improving their motor skills, whether by climbing on furniture, racing around the house, or going upstairs, downstairs, inside, or outside. It doesn't matter; they just need to be busy. Also, fine motor movements are being mastered: handles have to be turned, jars opened, blocks built, papers cut. During this period things are not only knocked down, but can also be put back together. Dressing—putting on one's own socks and shoes, fastening buttons, and undoing zippers—is also of interest.

It is during these years that language skills develop by leaps and bounds. The child who began by putting simple sentences together can now use more complex ones. The question "Why?" is uttered over and over, and this simple, repeated word underlines that the child is becoming inquisitive. It is this curiosity that makes us human. During this time frame there continues to be great emotional development. Feelings toward the parents are deep, with warm and tender moments prominently displayed. However, children still want to assert themselves by acting out, and may even think they know best.

When a girl starts to identify with her mother, she may compete with her for the father's attention. A boy begins to realize that he is like his father and patterns himself accordingly. A lot of observing goes on, during which each child models him- or herself by gender identification. Gender stereotyping starts early even though parents may try to avoid it. Friends and relatives invariably reinforce gender rules by giving what are thought to be sex-appropriate gifts, e.g. dolls and kitchen sets for girls, and trucks, trains, and balls for boys. Interestingly, girls may often insist on dressing up, including with jewellery, while boys usually care little about their clothes, other than being "sporty". By the time school starts, gender identities are usually well established. Importantly, while reinforcing the gender identification, parents should encourage the best of human qualities in their children of either sex. Nurturing and empathy, traditionally thought to be female characteristics, are now recognized as important for all growing children, while self-assertiveness and adventurousness should not be just for boys.

Play is still a toddler's main goal in life. It is fun, releases energy, and allows the child to enjoy and control his/her emotions. During these years, the child not only plays, but, by doing so begins problem-solving and expressing him/herself. Physically, emotionally, and verbally, these are important skills to have over a lifetime.

During these early, formative years, children require discipline. Disciplining a child is one of the most important yet difficult aspects of parenthood. Parents often forget that they are not predominantly friends of their children; that will come later in life. Effective and positive discipline both guides and teaches children, providing structure and boundaries for their lives. Within established confines, the child feels safe, secure, and protected. Out of consistent and fair discipline, children learn self-control, respect for those responsible for them, and important values for their lifetimes. Discipline should be for a specific incident and proportional to the misbehaviour. Rules must apply equally to siblings. Consistency is critical. Harsh discipline, such as name-calling, shouting, or humiliation should never be used. Never ever should parents or others physically harm a child. Children must understand that it is their behaviour that is in question, not your love for them. Parents have a unique bond with their children; they must encourage and praise good behaviour, yet provide fair discipline when warranted. Positive reinforcement ultimately leads to healthy mental development and respect for authoritative figures.

YOUNGSTER: AGE FOUR TO FIVE
"Out on My Own."

During the ages of four to five, you are no longer an infant or a toddler. You've been told that you are a "big girl" or a "big boy" now. Your parents want you to believe in the positive aspects of getting older, and you also want to prove that you can be big and can do things for yourself. You want to dress yourself, eat what you want, play on your own, and choose for yourself what you want to do.

Four-year-olds often "know it all". They can be outspoken, aggressive with their playmates, talkative, self-absorbed, and insensitive to others. These are all concerning behavioural issues. This can be a difficult stage, but children do enjoy being with others the same age and truly, deeply want friends.

Early Childhood

During these first four years of life you have had a huge growth spurt—physically, mentally, and emotionally. You have mastered motor skills and now are well coordinated. You can walk, run, jump, skip and hop, as well as throw and catch a ball. Your strength is demonstrated on the climbing frame with all its activities. Fine motor movements are almost fully developed. You can brush your teeth and hair; use a spoon, fork, and knife; cut paper; and start doing crafts. How fun it is to master building sets! Language skills have grown, so that you can now easily explain things and express yourself. During these years fantasy can be confused with reality, based on your healthy imagination. Your attention span grows; you can listen to stories and understand what is spoken and read to you.

Parents are still the most critical part of your social interactions, but playmates come a close second. You are becoming social, preferring to play with others rather than on your own or just with your own family. You want a play date. With increasing confidence, you enjoy striking out on your own, testing the boundaries. Unfortunately, you can be aggressive with other children, and need to learn about sharing and taking turns with your friends and others.

Youngster: Age Four to Five

It is during the early formative years that one hopes you learn about the true value of reading. You see other family members reading papers, books, manuals, and computer screens. Hopefully your parents will first introduce you to picture books and, when you're ready, more advanced books with interesting stories. Over time, books with facts become important, so you can begin to learn about your new world. Reading is one of the greatest gifts parents, family, and our society can provide to young minds. With any luck, a wholesome desire to learn develops and becomes life-long. Now you are ready for school.

Chapter Three

SCHOOL AGE: AGE FIVE TO TEN

"I'm off to school!"

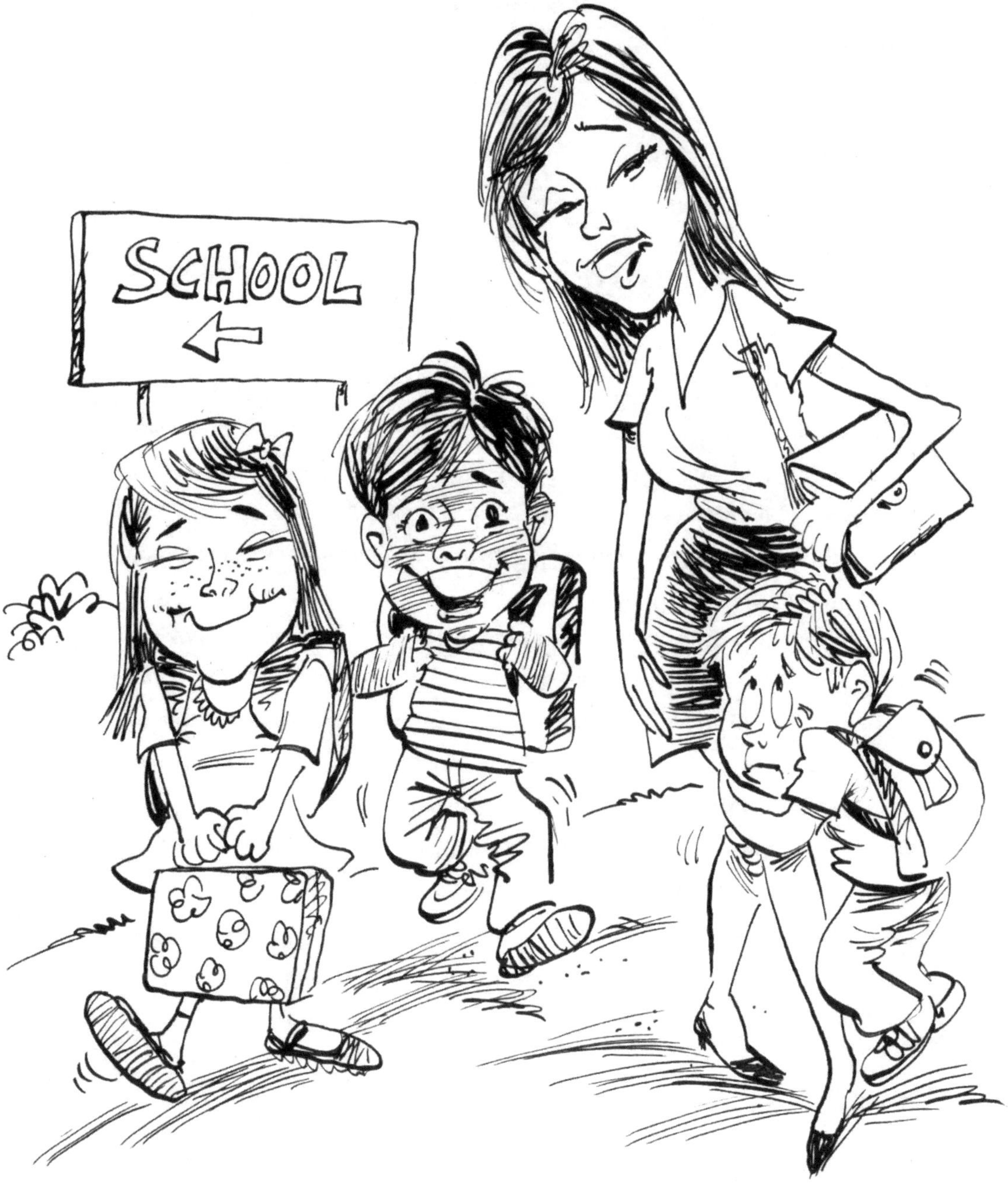
SCHOOL

SCHOOL
"I Don't Want to Go!"

By the age of five or six, you are no longer a young child, but in more common terms, you're a "kid." As you grow older, you become more social, need your parents less, and want to be with people your own age. The most important thing to you is your relationship with other kids with the same interests. You not only want to be accepted by them, but you are concerned about what they think of you and what they say.

When you start school, you want to seem independent from your parents. Although at this stage you are totally dependent on them for the basics of life, you don't like to admit it and can be visibly "cooler" to your mom and dad. You don't want to be seen as needing your parents but want to stand on your own, or at least try to appear so to your playmates.

Children at this age begin questioning their parents, often believing other people's opinions rather than their mom and dad's. A child can become impatient with the family and reject or ignore comments or wise advice.

It is during these early years of schooling that the young may pick up bad attitudes. Unfortunately, they learn in the schoolyard not only tough talk, but often unacceptable language, becoming rude and pushy, and challenging what parents have tried to teach them earlier at home. Parents can be troubled by this rebellious phase.

However difficult, parents should accept and welcome this growth towards independence, yet be very mindful if and when it turns nasty or hurtful to others. It is best to be aware that their child is "testing the waters". What's important is that the child is gaining confidence. Parents, teachers, and other adults must step back, and be light-hearted about these early attempts of their children to stand on their own. What is most important is to be firm when required, so as to prevent children from thinking that they are in control and can do and say whatever they want. Big mistake if the child and the parents think they are on an equal footing! A recipe for disaster!

School Age: Age Five to Ten

MY SOCIAL LIFE
"I Like You."

Nothing seems more important than to be accepted by children of your own age. No child wants to feel isolated. Your parents should encourage you to befriend others and play with children your own age. It becomes important to you to dress like them, talk like them, and try to be as similar to them as possible. This can be fine as long as those outward choices are considered acceptable. Obviously, parents should guard against children and situations that would be considered bad influences on you.

Early on, children tend to form groups. This aspect of socialization can be good, as it strengthens their feeling of self-worth. But too often this grouping (or clique) can lead to destructive behaviour by excluding other children. In the schoolyard, ganging up can often have very hurtful results, and even end in physical violence. Over time, as the child gets older, cliques can form based on superficial criteria such as physical beauty, athletic ability, clothing, money, or academic performance. If a child happens to have none of these "desirable" features, he/she may feel isolated and ashamed, which can often lead to depression. It is the job of parents, teachers and school communities to step in and help alleviate the situation. Every individual has his or her own strengths. It is important to find these and to promote and showcase them.

BULLIES
"Get Out of My Way!"

Unfortunately, people who bully have always been part of the school environment. Years ago, it was believed that one had to learn to deal with these unpleasant, manipulative individuals and tolerate them as best as one could, as part of growing up. Tragically, bullies target the most vulnerable children, causing humiliation, fear, and loneliness in the often shy and less confident students. It is extremely destructive behaviour, which, today, is considered totally unacceptable.

Parents, families, and schools must have a zero tolerance for such behaviour. Prevention must be the priority. Although those on the receiving end suffer the greatest, we now know that bullies themselves can, and often do, suffer lifelong consequences for their behaviour. Although the bully thinks that he or she prospers through intimidation of others, follow-up studies show that they will likely have difficulty with normal relationships in the long term. Underneath the façade of a strong exterior, they are usually insecure and troubled individuals. They mask that by picking on others for one reason or another. In later life these bullies have fewer friends, often have difficulty holding a job, and may become entangled with the law. Victims of bullying need all the support we can give. Bullies need discipline and education about their troubling behaviour. The earlier the intervention, the better for all concerned. For everyone's sake, bullying is something that should not and cannot be tolerated.

CHILDHOOD RESPONSIBILITIES
"Who, Me—Work?"

Years ago—and still today in some societies, children have had responsibilities to their wider family. Kids born in poorer parts of the world participate in helping the family earn a living, whether on farms or in small businesses or factories. In our more developed world, such as North America and Europe, school has become the child's main "occupation". Sophisticated societies place a great deal of emphasis on formal education and instil in the child a duty to succeed.

This doesn't mean that you shouldn't contribute at home by helping out in some small way. It is important for you to have certain duties. Initially simple tasks such as setting the table, taking out the garbage, or walking the dog can be helpful. Over time, you will be able to graduate to more skilled tasks like cooking, cleaning, or mowing the lawn. This is not only a valuable help to your parents, but helps to develop useful skills. Allowances teach children how to manage money. Receiving spending money may be part of how your parents educate you about how the real world works. Whether or not you should be rewarded for simple chores is an open question. Certainly, if you make a special effort it is not unreasonable to negotiate a bonus!

Homework for school requires discipline and is also part of self-improvement. In the early years of school, homework is meant to provide an opportunity for independent study and to practice what you are learning in school. It should not be a burden at this early stage of primary school. Playing and socializing afterwards is equally important. There should be some free time for sports and other things of interest, e.g. music, ballet, etc., which should also be part of your overall development.

Chapter Four

PUBERTY: AGE TEN TO FIFTEEN

"Wow! What's Happening to Me?"

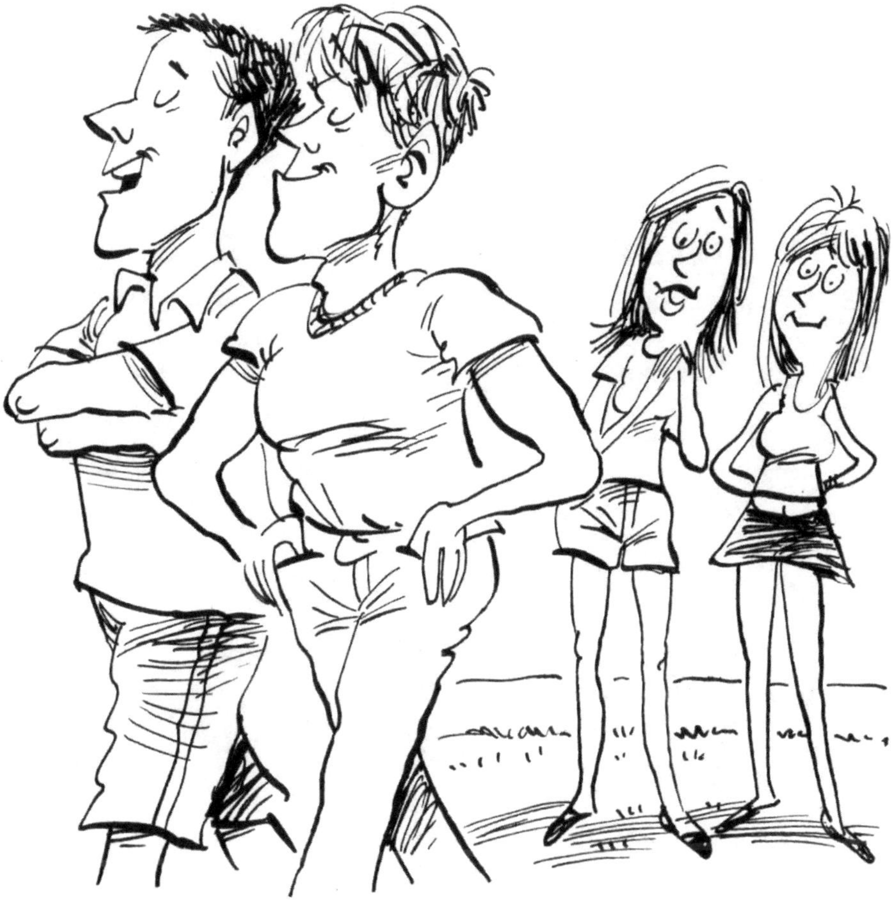

PHYSICAL CHANGES

You have been a child for as long as you can remember. You have been growing up, first from a toddler to a child, then to a kid, at about four to five centimeters (two inches) per year. Suddenly, you notice things beginning to change, either in yourself or your friends. Almost overnight, physical changes occur. First you notice that your clothes no longer fit. Your growth rate increases, doubling to nine to ten centimeters (four to five inches) a year, and you feel hungry all the time. Your body begins to change noticeably, and you start to think differently—often about the opposite sex. These physical and mental changes are the first signs of your puberty. It is the time in our lives when we begin maturing and are on our way to becoming adults. During puberty, each of us completes our development so that we will eventually be able to have children ourselves.

Puberty: Age Ten to Fifteen

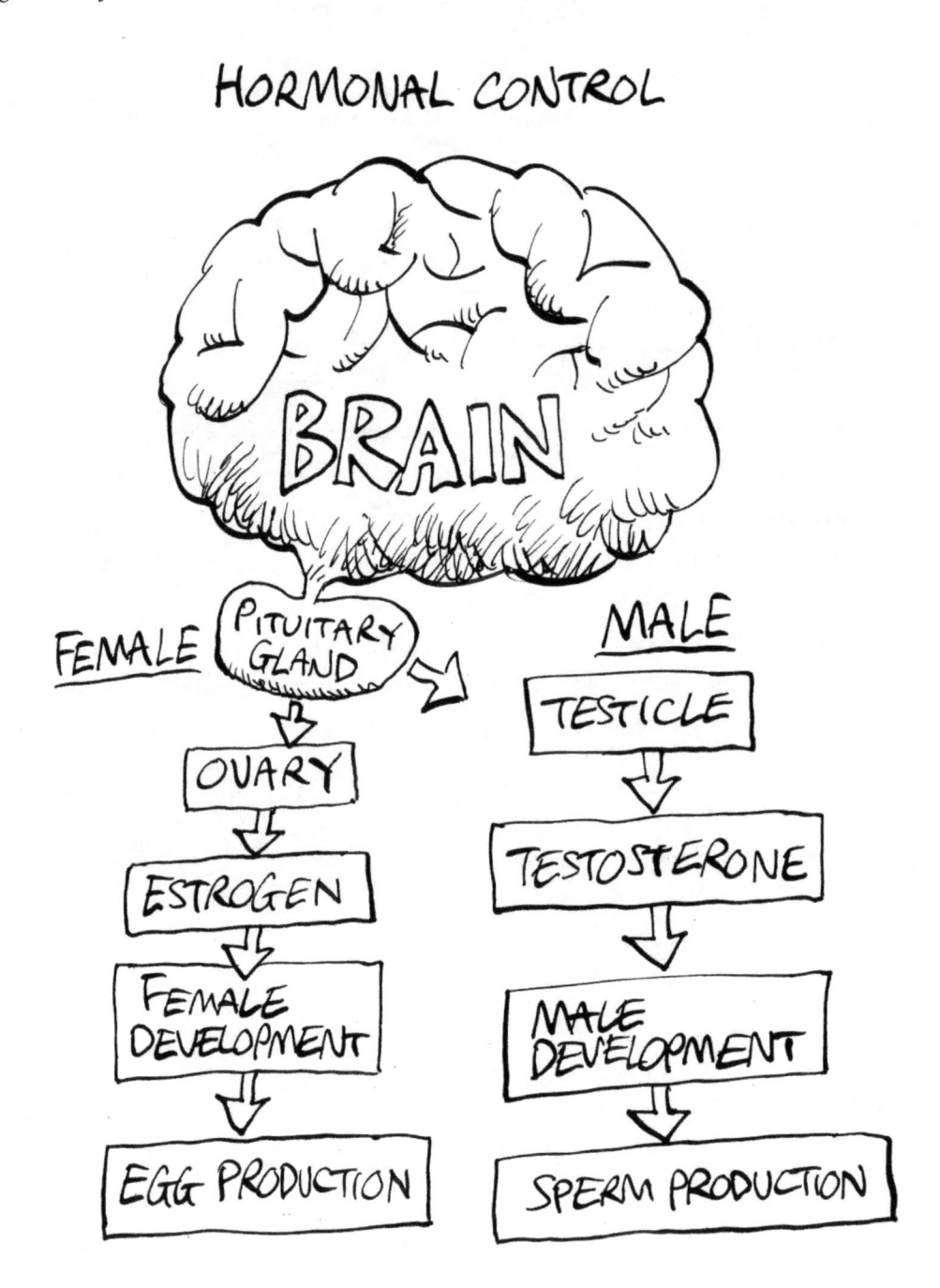

HORMONAL CONTROL

FEMALE

BRAIN → PITUITARY GLAND → OVARY → ESTROGEN → FEMALE DEVELOPMENT → EGG PRODUCTION

MALE

TESTICLE → TESTOSTERONE → MALE DEVELOPMENT → SPERM PRODUCTION

Puberty is genetically controlled, but influenced by many other factors. Nutrition, body weight, and body fat play a significant role in helping to trigger this event. As well, race, culture, socio-economic status, and physical activity are all implicated in triggering or delaying the onset of puberty. Controlling all of this is the master gland of the body: the pituitary gland, located at the base of the brain. The pituitary gland releases hormones that travel in the bloodstream to activate the adrenal glands and the ovaries in the female, and the adrenal glands and testicles in the male. These organs then produce estrogen, which dominates female development, and the potent hormone testosterone, which accounts for male development. The timing of one's own maturation can vary, but whether early or late, it happens to everyone, and we can't change that, no matter what we think or might wish.

Puberty: Age Ten to Fifteen

FEMALE DEVELOPMENT

Most girls first notice a "tingling", first under one nipple, then the other, and the formation of a small, firm "button" of early breast tissue just below the nipple. This usually occurs around the age of ten, but can be earlier or later and still considered normal. Breast development is influenced by estrogen, produced from both ovaries. Accompanying breast development is a rapid growth in height—from four to five centimeters (two inches) per year before puberty, to ten centimeters (four to five inches) or more after the onset.

Puberty: Age Ten to Fifteen

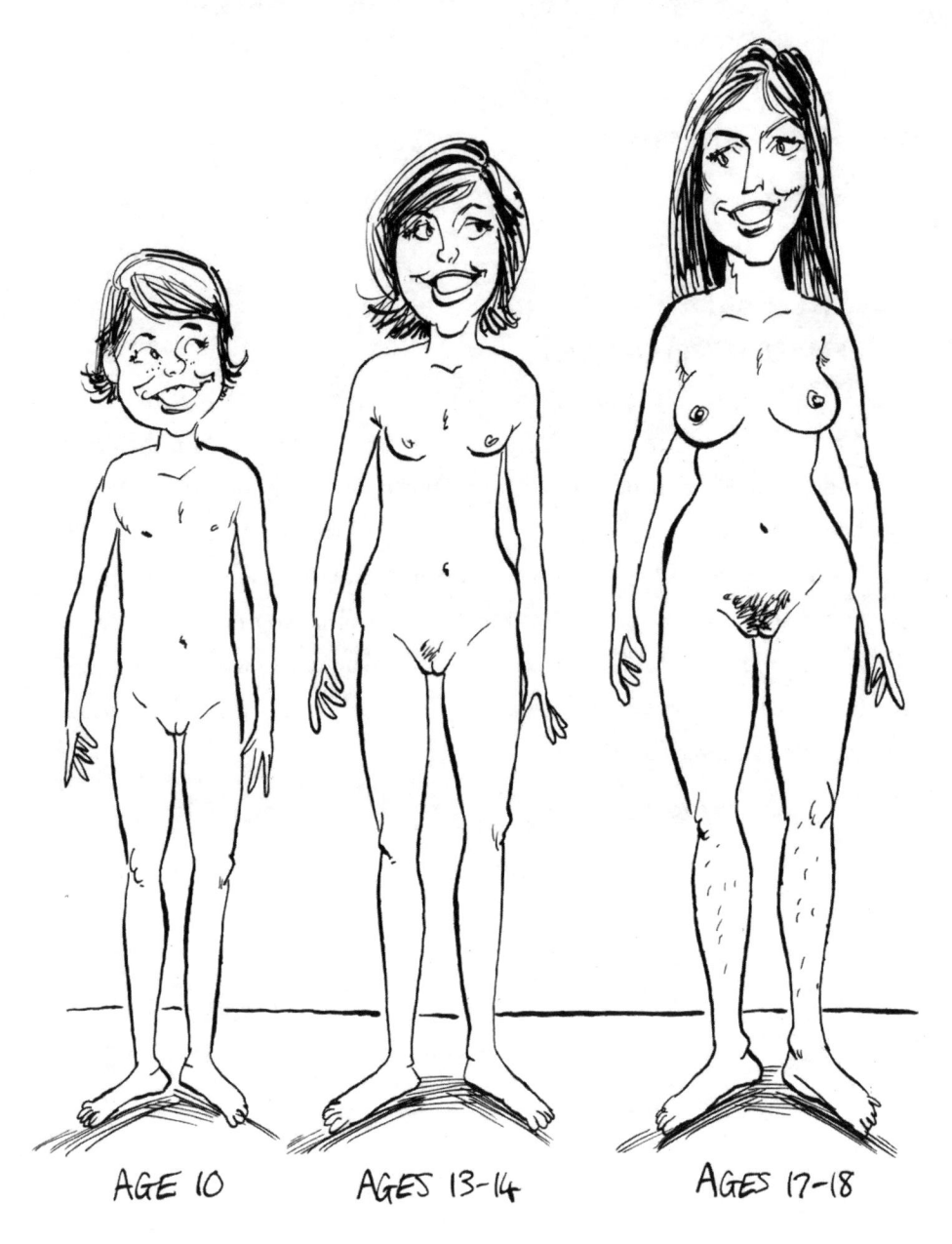

Weight changes are also noticed; from two to three kilos (five to eight pounds) per year before puberty begins, to four to eight kilos (ten to twenty pounds) per year during this rapid growth phase. Breast development continues, first with small, firm, cone-like breasts that may be unequal in size. Ultimately, the nipples enlarge, become elevated from the breast itself, and over time the breasts round out and become hemispheric.

Puberty: Age Ten to Fifteen

Along with structural growth and breast maturation, pubic (lower abdomen) and axillary hair (under the arms), appear. Coinciding with this, certain skin changes occur, often resulting in pimples or acne formation. These features are the result of small amounts of androgens, male hormones, normally produced in the girl's adrenal glands.

Puberty: Age Ten to Fifteen

Hips widen and the body contour is rounded by the formation of additional fat. Most girls don't like the idea of having increased body fat, but more fat is normal and important to initiate and support the young girl's first period when she notes some external bleeding from her vagina into her underwear. (More on that later). An adequate amount of body fat is critical for the development of regular periods.

Regular, predictable monthly periods indicate a young girl is beginning to ovulate (release an egg). It is during this last phase of puberty that the young girl begins to ovulate, usually fourteen days before her next period.

Normally, the pubertal girl has her first period about two to two-and-a-half years after initial breast budding, but regular ovulatory cycles start months to years later, depending on other factors referred to earlier. Once regular ovulation occurs in this post-pubertal girl, she is physically and sexually mature and can have her own child, ready or not!

Puberty: Age Ten to Fifteen

MALE SEXUAL DEVELOPMENT

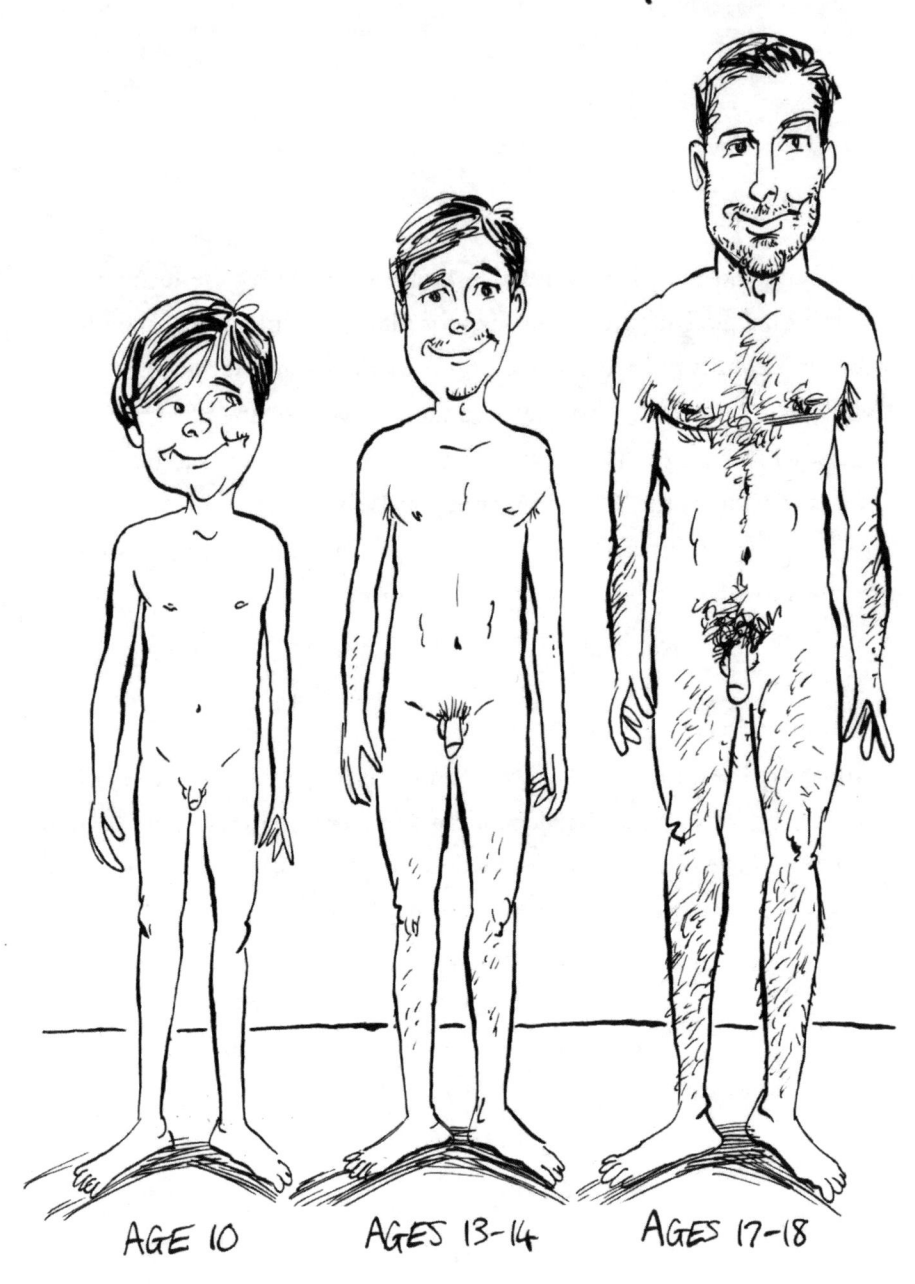

AGE 10   AGES 13-14   AGES 17-18

MALE DEVELOPMENT

A boy's pubertal development begins about two years after the average female's, but may have a wider age range at the start and at completion; usually between ages eleven to eighteen. Its onset is not as dramatic or as obvious as breast growth in females. The first sign of puberty for males is testicular enlargement, the onset of pubic hair, and growth of the penis, both in length and width. Following these genital developments, the boy's real growth spurt can be dramatic, reaching up to twelve centimeters (five to six inches) per year, at least doubling the rate observed in childhood. Accompanying this growth in height is the remarkable lengthening of both arms and legs and an increase in foot size. These developments can give the impression of a gangling young man having funny proportions and perhaps appearing uncoordinated.

Following these initial structural changes, more hair appears on a young man's body: under his arms and on the face, where it becomes darker, coarser, thicker, and longer. He considers that it might be time to start shaving. His voice begins to crack and become deeper as the larynx, or voice box, enlarges. All these changes are the results of androgenic hormones being released from both the testicles and adrenal glands. Some boys may also note breast enlargement and tenderness, the result of a small amount of estrogen production. This effect on the male's breasts is short-lived, but can be a cause for embarrassment and concern in those young males experiencing it.

The male's pubertal growth can take years to complete, sometimes into the late teens, before a final height is achieved. Interestingly, boys who have their pubertal development at a younger age will complete their growth earlier than those who start later. The earlier developers often end up shorter than those whose puberty was delayed. Body odour and acne are caused by male hormones, and can be managed satisfactorily, but care is required to avoid secondary infection in acne sufferers.

During puberty and its prolonged growth phase, boys will notice an increasing number of penile erections, when the penis fills with blood, making it firm. During sleep, these young men will begin having "wet dreams," when they ejaculate a fluid from the penis. This is the first visible sign of sperm production, which needs to be released.

Sperm production, under hormonal control, is the sign indicating full maturation and the completion of sexual and physical development. The male now has the ability to father a child.

Chapter Five

ADOLESCENCE: AGE TWELVE TO EIGHTEEN

"I feel different!"

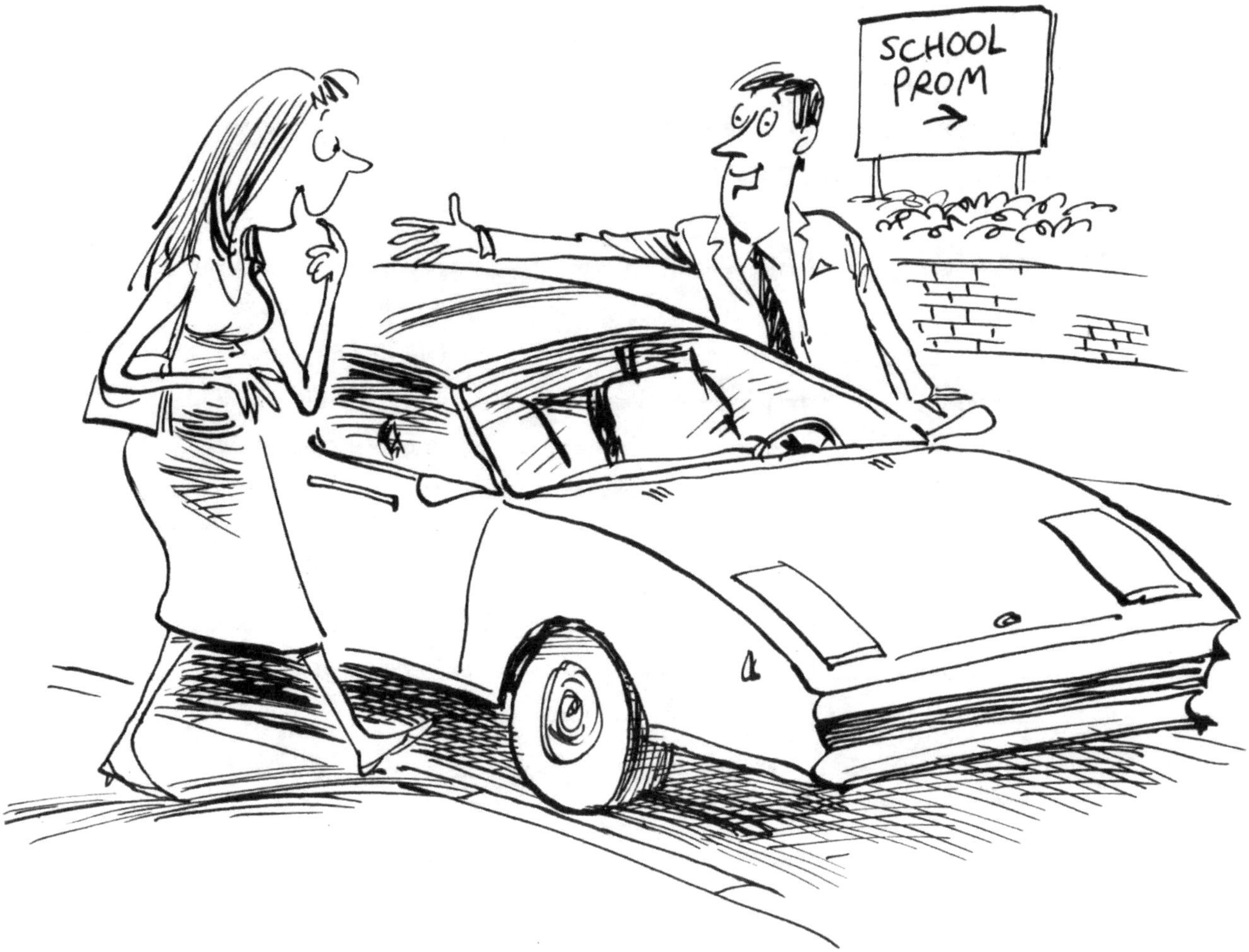
SCHOOL
PROM

SEXUAL, EMOTIONAL, AND INTELLECTUAL DEVELOPMENT

"Adolescence" refers to the time when a young person begins to become an adult. This dramatic growth phase involves not only the physical changes of puberty, but also the immense mental and psychological development that's undergone in the progress towards emotional maturity. It is a time in teenagers' lives when they search for true independence from their parents and family. At the same time, parents and other family members reluctantly have to let go, which can lead to tensions.

This can be an especially turbulent time, both for you and for your mom and dad, but it is a most necessary one. While you want to be free from your close family in order to follow your own path and dreams, your parents, deep down, want this for you as well. The problems arise when there are marked differences between your actions or the choices you have made and what your parents believe would be best for you.

EARLY ADOLESCENCE

The onset of puberty, as previously discussed, is the marker for the beginning of adolescence. As mentioned earlier, body changes usually occur around or after the age of ten in girls and twelve in boys, but there can be a wide variation within and between the sexes. This variability can cause anxiety for the teen who starts early or develops late. The important fact, however, is to recognize that you and all your peers will reach adulthood during these adolescent years. Young people are acutely self-conscious about their bodies and think that their friends and others are focused on them. Freckles, acne, weight gain, body hair, and rapid or slow growth all play on a young person's mind.

Many young teenagers desperately try to conform to their classmates, whether in dress, haircut or hairstyle, speech, music, or whatever seems important at the time. They want to be the same as their peers, but each generation also wants to be different from an earlier one. It's not unusual for young people to reject and feel somewhat ashamed of their parents. Not only do they want to be different from their parents, but they also want to be better and, specifically, "cooler."

LATE ADOLESCENCE

Over time, this growing up gets more difficult and challenging. You have staked your claim on your own independence, but you are beginning to appreciate that the world is real and not easy, and that you have difficult decisions to make. You become uncertain. You have left the protected and dependent early years of being a youngster, where you had been shielded from the harsh reality of day-to-day life. Now, being more and more on your own, you can feel an inner turmoil, if not outright fear. It might begin to seem to you that you are not as smart as you thought you were. Others appear to do much better in school, and many of your friends seem to manage their life situations better than you can.

There is no going back in life, so you must continue to move forward, as hard as this is when you feel uncertain, distracted, or outright lost. You begin to recognize that you have to find a firm footing and a path that suits you. Each of us has to stop pretending, search deep within ourselves, reassess, and finally recognize who we are and who we wish to become. This takes time and honesty as you toss out many unrealistic expectations and focus on your real abilities, strengths and weaknesses. You recognize that you must build your life based on accepting your limitations and the supports available to you. Am I a person to follow an academic path to a professional career, or would it be better to follow a less intellectual course? What resources do I have and what might be available to me? How am I going to manage once I leave my parents' home?

Adolescence: Age Twelve to Eighteen

From our experiences at school during our earlier years, we will have been either encouraged or discouraged about our potential. However, students who have had a harder time with their early education need not abandon their hopes and dreams and stop striving. Many of us are late bloomers and only find what we really enjoy and are good at later in life. "If there's a will there's a way." It just takes dedication and hard work to succeed.

The most difficult aspect of adolescence to achieve is emotional maturity. Many factors, some negative and some positive, influence this maturity. We are all dealt a certain hand at birth that is further shaped by life's experiences. Importantly, we want and need to feel loved and respected. Our family situation is paramount! Whether we've had a traditional upbringing with both parents, been raised by a single parent (mother or father), or were adopted, our home circumstances are influential. One's economic situation, although important, is not critical to ultimate success. Many of the world's most respected individuals came from humble beginnings. Curiosity, exposure to various aspects of life, and intellectual stimulation in the family unit are important factors, but also, any stimulation from the wider community contributes to one's development. Our race and culture have a great influence on us as well. No doubt the quality of our schools and our teachers is also paramount to our intellectual future, influencing who we are and who we will become.

Each of us must recognize and accept our own personal realities and work through our unique situations and "baggage". We must acknowledge, deep down, both the positives and negatives of our lives and build from that.

No one is like you. You are who you are. Like it or not, each of us must do our best to reach our own potential and goals. It is unlikely that you will be given the Nobel Prize, or become a world champion or internationally famous, but each of us can become important and successful and can contribute in some small way.

THE HARD-TO-DO

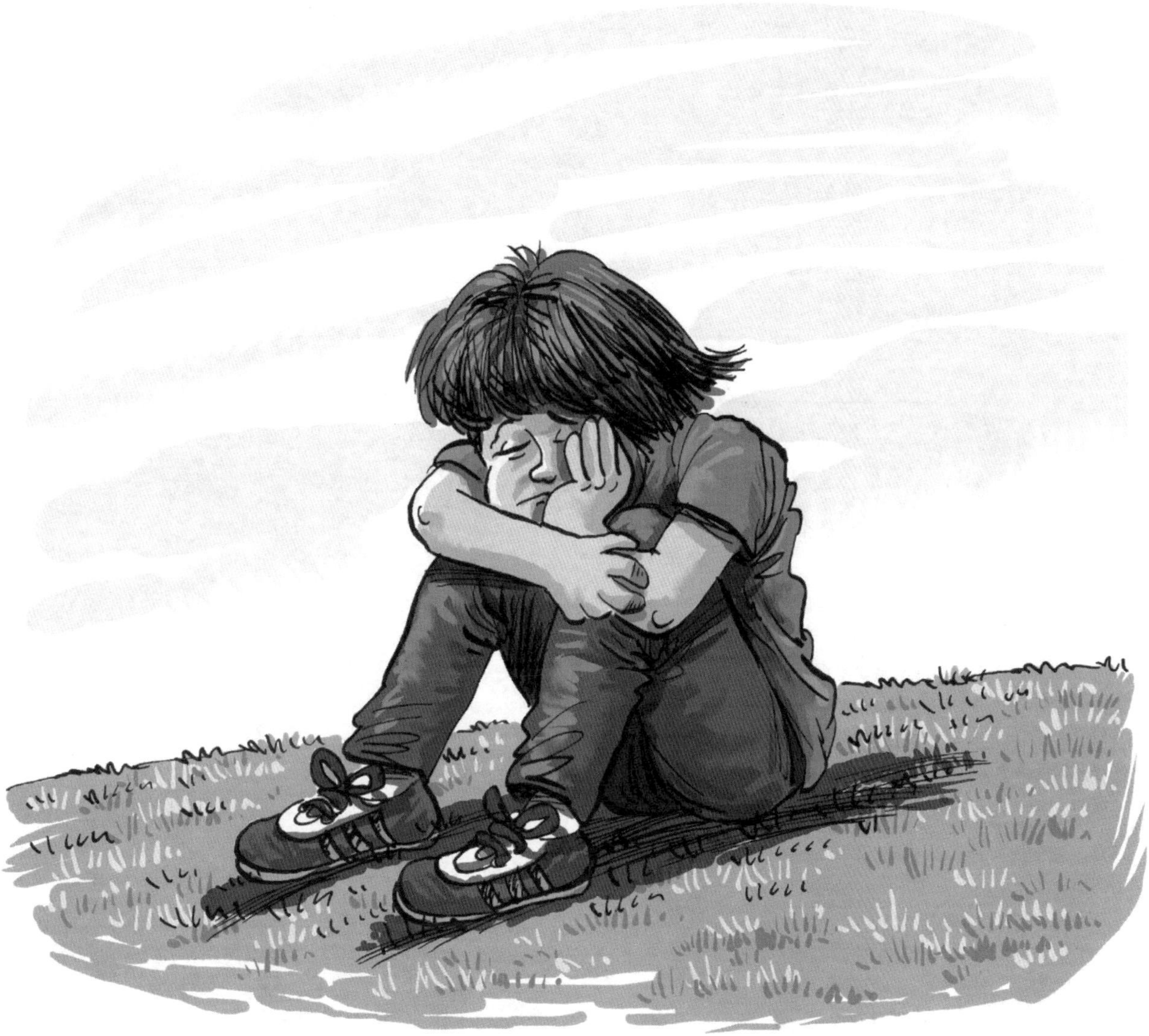

Chapter Six

SEX

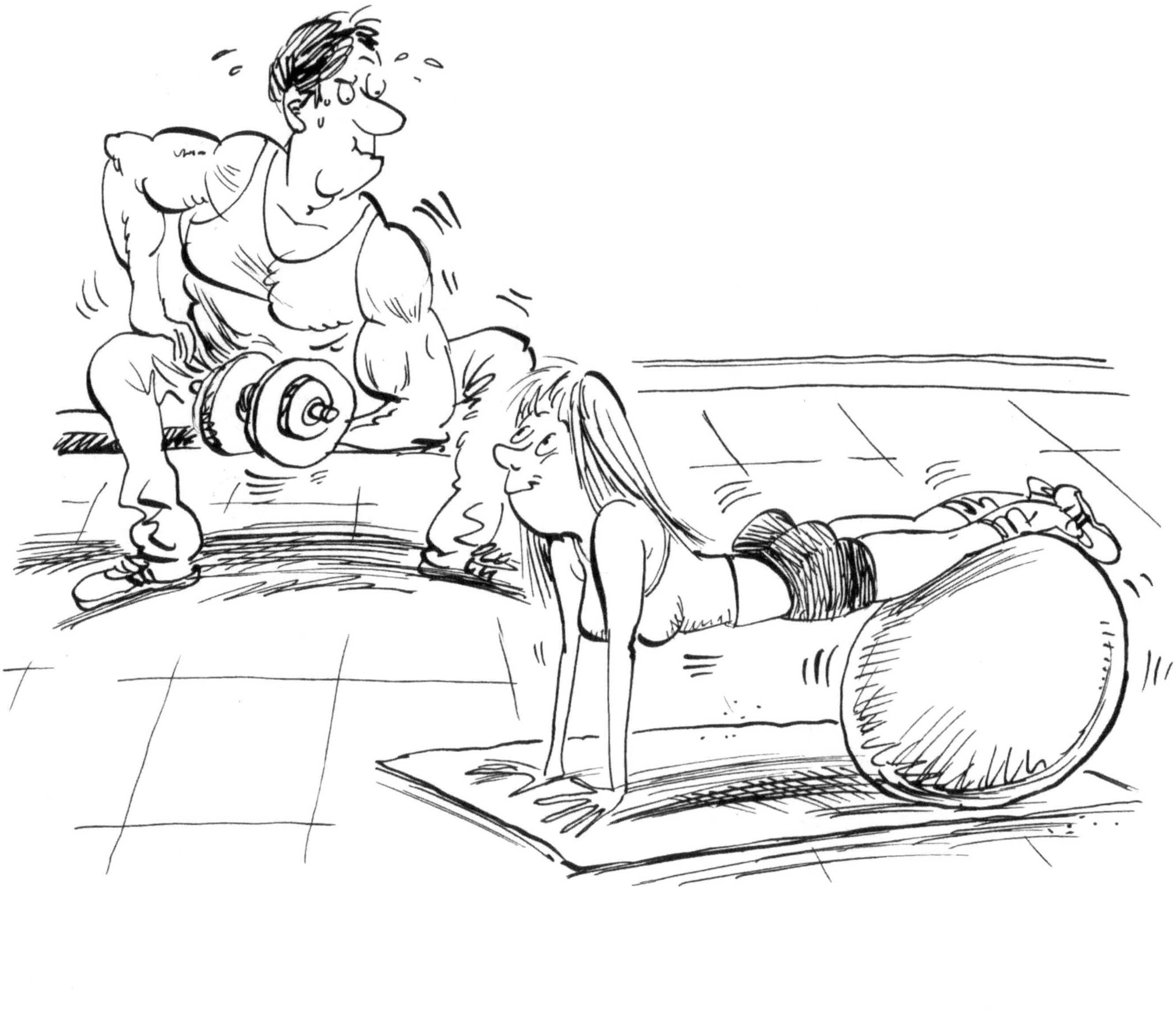

SEXUAL IDENTITY

We are sexual beings, from when we first come into the world at conception, until we die. Our sexuality is inborn, an essential part of who we are. When a sperm from your father unites with an egg from your mother, you become biologically either a male or a female. All sperm carry two sex chromosomes, an X and a Y, whereas the female egg has two X's. If the Y-chromosome from your father fuses with either X chromosome from your mother, then you will be a boy. If your father passes on his only X chromosome, then you will develop into a girl. The Y chromosome directs development along male lines, with the formation of two testicles, a prostate, and a penis. If no Y chromosome is present, then the development is female, comprising a vulva, vagina, uterus, and two ovaries.

Sex

GENITAL DEVELOPMENT

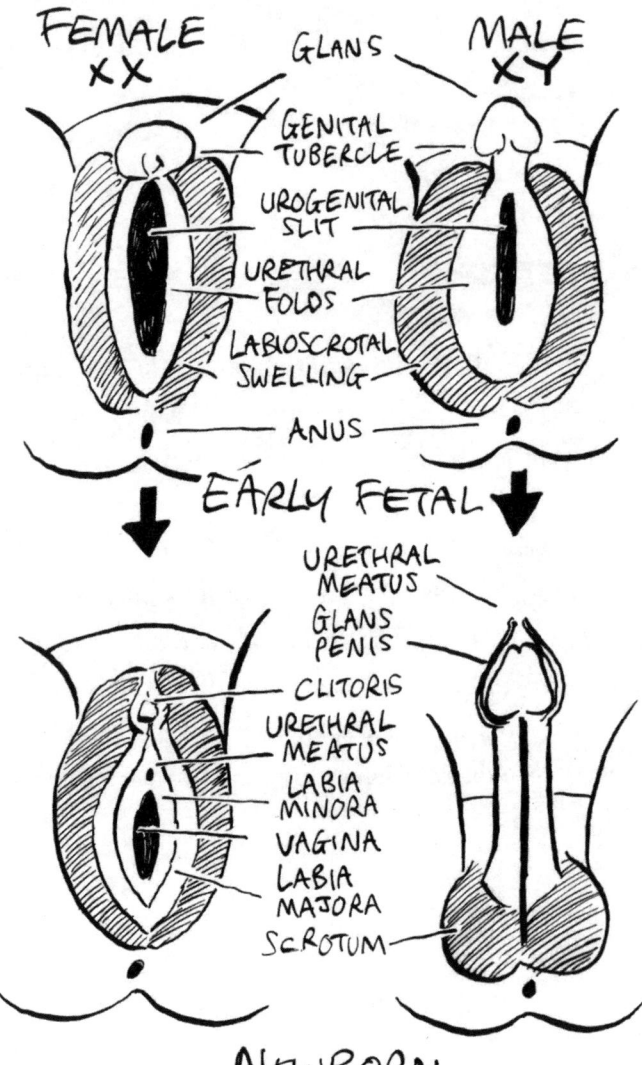

FEMALE XX — **MALE XY**

- GLANS
- GENITAL TUBERCLE
- UROGENITAL SLIT
- URETHRAL FOLDS
- LABIOSCROTAL SWELLING
- ANUS

EARLY FETAL

- URETHRAL MEATUS
- GLANS PENIS
- CLITORIS
- URETHRAL MEATUS
- LABIA MINORA
- VAGINA
- LABIA MAJORA
- SCROTUM

NEWBORN

IT'S A GIRL!   IT'S A BOY!

Sexual Identity

Our sexual identities, though, are much more complex. When we are born, our sex is announced by whoever attends the birth. We are either little girls or little boys, established by observing the external appearance of our genitalia. As previously noted, this most important decision on sex assignment is made in a matter of seconds by a complete stranger!

Most children have a very clear sense of whether they are boys or girls from a very young age; certainly by the age of two. In spite of our best efforts, parents, family, friends and the wider society treat boys and girls differently, however subtly. Boys are expected to be more active, play with trucks and balls, dress more casually, and be more difficult to manage. Girls, on the other hand, are thought to be more reserved, enjoy quieter play with dolls and crafts, and be more easily managed, at least initially.

However, our true sex, either male or female, can be based on and influenced by other considerations. In addition to our "Chromosomal Sex" and the "External Genitalia Sex", many other aspects can come into play. Our "Internal Sexual Organs" usually match our external genitalia, but not always. How we are raised by our families and our wider society is critical and ingrains in us a "Brain Sex". Next, during puberty, comes our "Hormonal Sex," reinforcing and changing our bodies and thought processes. Ultimately, our gender comes down to our "Psychological Sex": how we view ourselves and which sex we are attracted to. For nearly all of us, all these various aspects of our sexuality match. We are either males or females and most often attracted to the opposite sex. But some of us don't feel this way and struggle to discover who we really are sexually, and then deal with that aspect of our lives.

Humans are sensual beings; enjoying taste, touch, sounds and feelings of warmth. Pleasure is critical to our wellbeing. Over time, infants and young children recognize pleasure by touching their genitalia. They become curious, noting the difference between themselves and playmates of the opposite sex—why do some kids have a penis and others don't? Playing doctor and "show and tell" are all part of early learning about one's sexuality.

Puberty changes everything. Before puberty, our lives are simpler. We are young, protected, and hopefully loved within a family and within a known social environment of friends, school, and a wider society that is relatively constant and predictable. Then along comes puberty, which changes everything; activating the ovaries in girls, and testicles in boys.

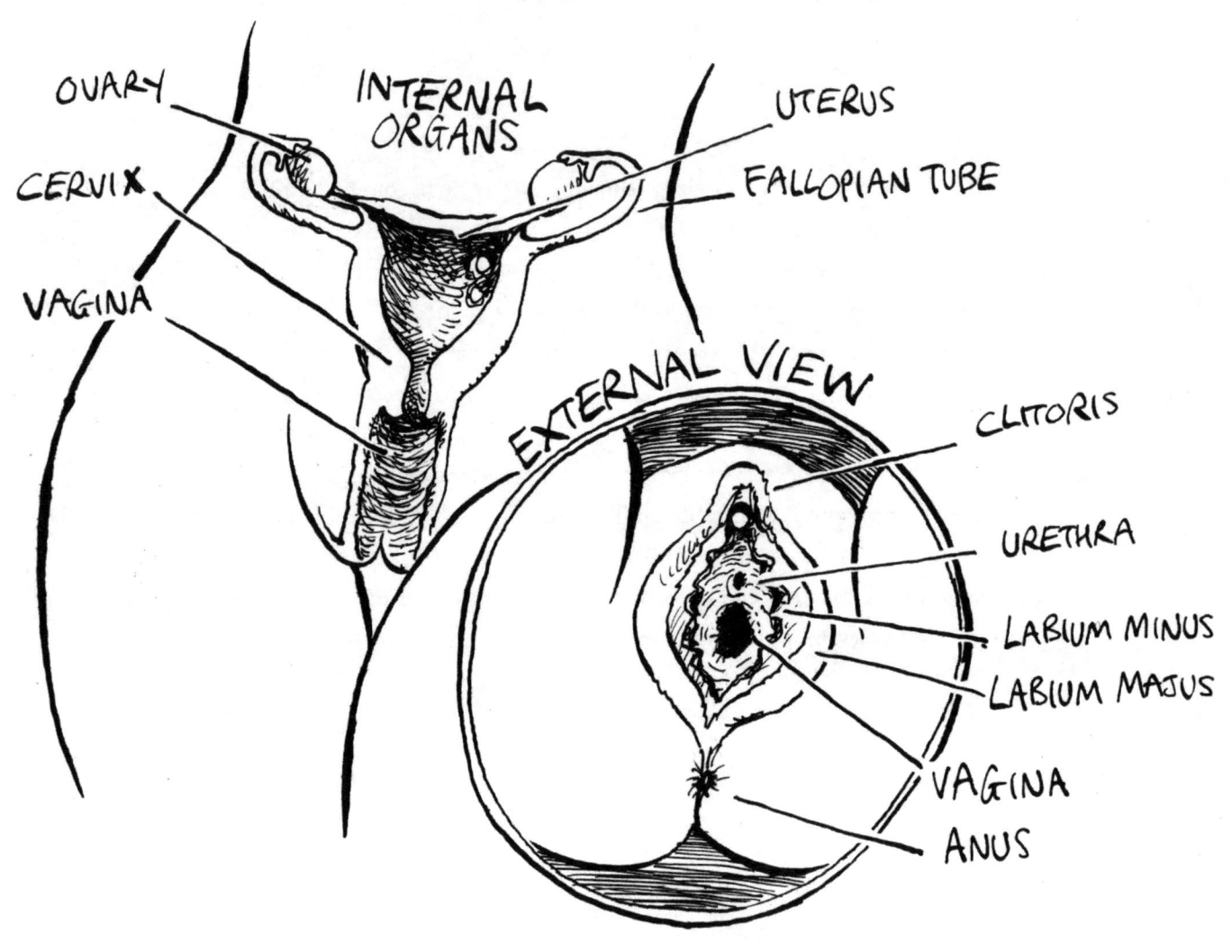

Sex

FEMALE

Girls are born with two ovaries: one on either side of the uterus. The ovaries produce two hormones, estrogen and progesterone, and also store all the girl's eggs for her entire reproductive life. At puberty, the brain, acting through the pituitary (a small gland at its base), releases specific hormones to activate the ovaries. Initially, only estrogen is released, which causes not only physical growth in height and weight, but also breast development and skeletal changes, as well as fat deposition. Most importantly, these hormones change how a young girl thinks, feels, and acts. Girls change from children with playful thoughts to maturing adolescents, often thinking more about boys, new relationships, love, their place in the world, or perhaps having a family.

Sex

MALE REPRODUCTIVE ORGANS

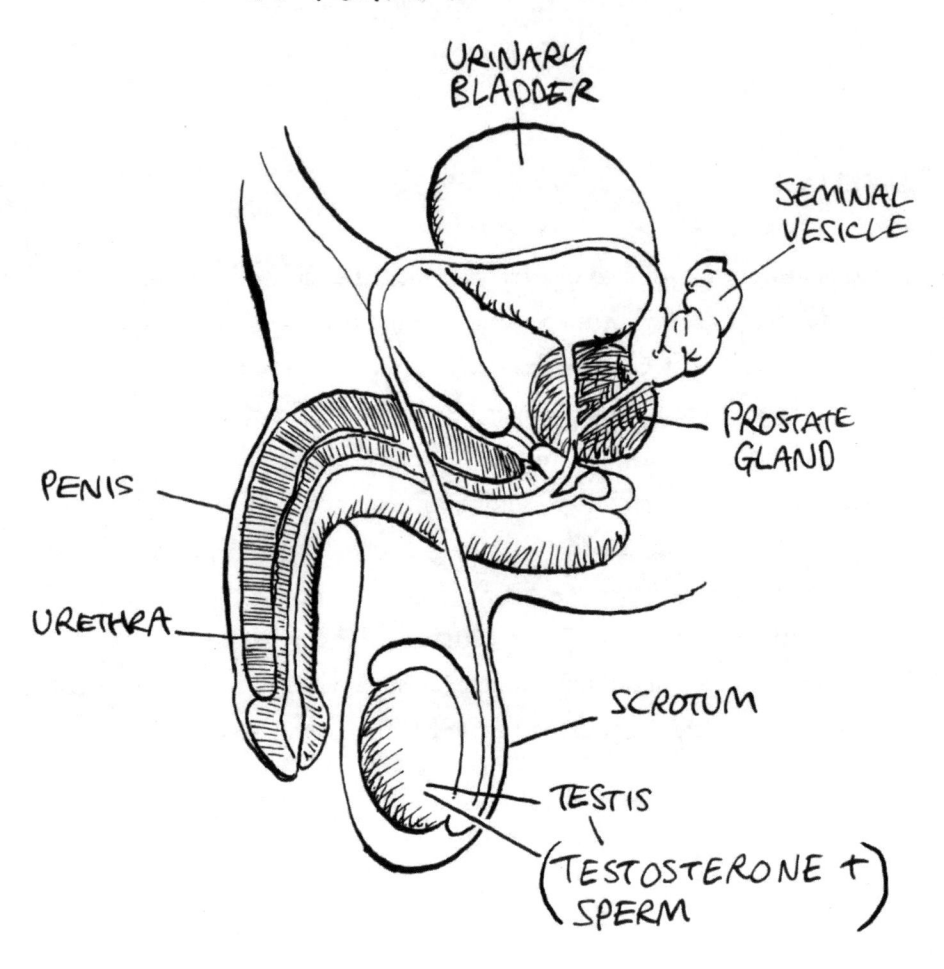

MALE

Boys are born with two testicles, one on either side of the scrotum, which is a closed sac found below and behind the penis. Testicles produce sperm cells and male hormones, testosterone being the most potent. At puberty, the testicles—again activated through the brain and pituitary gland—secrete testosterone and other male hormones, which give rise to a marked growth spurt, penile and testicular enlargement, body hair, acne, body odour, and sometimes an increase in aggressive behaviour.

Sex

LIFE'S EMBARRASSING MOMENTS!

In addition, the testicles begin to produce sperm. Accompanying this is an increasing frequency of erections, wherein blood flows to the penis, causing it to enlarge and stiffen up, often to the concern and embarrassment of the adolescent. Not infrequently, boys experience "wet dreams" or begin to masturbate, or stimulate their own penis. Releasing sperm relieves built-up sexual tension. During this time of marked change, boys also notice a change from their predictable lives by being and feeling different. At this point, they may become more interested in girls. Adolescent boys may become focused on the female body and the changes they witness, particularly in girls' breast development. The female figure often captures their imaginations.

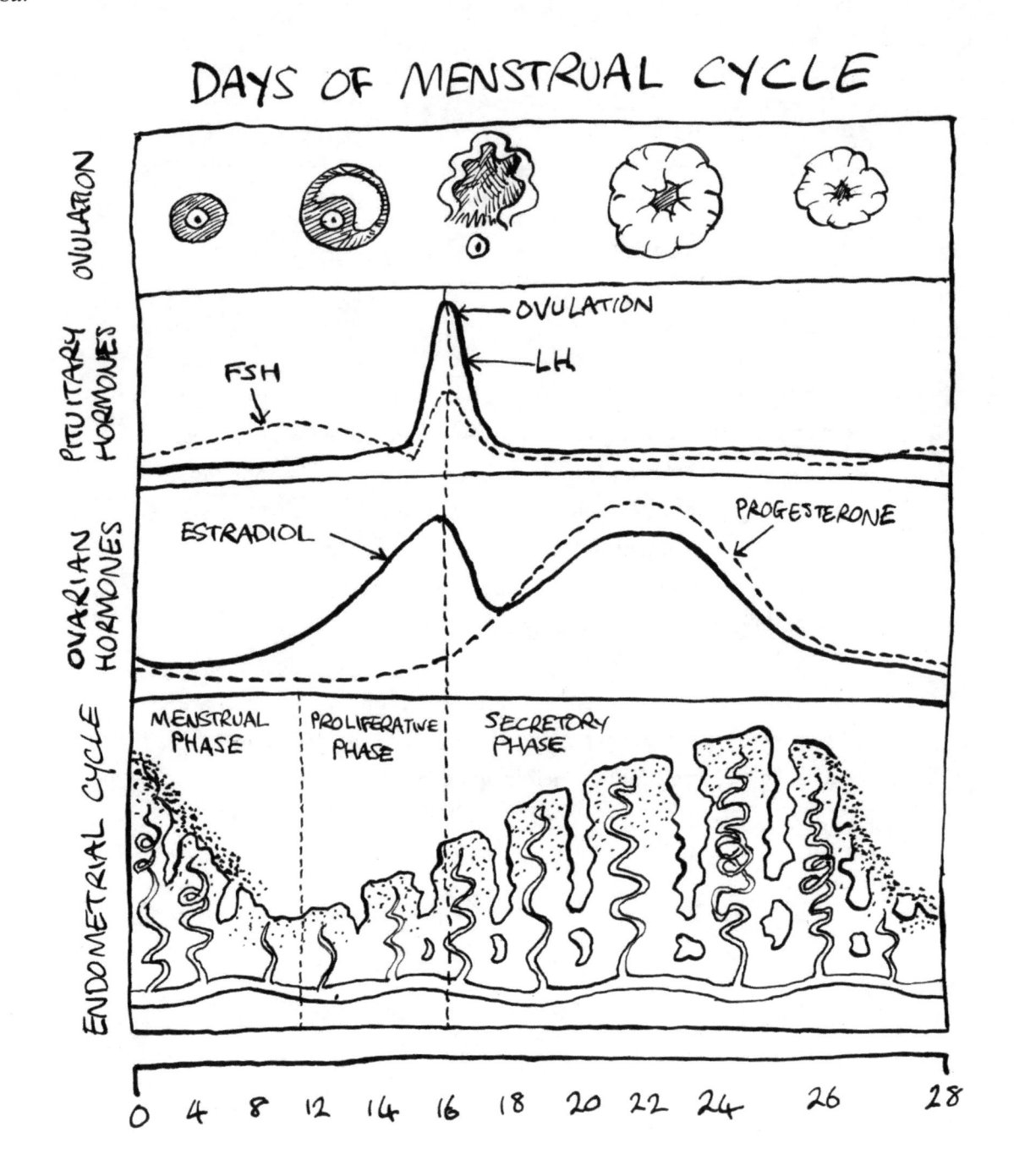

Sex

THE BIRDS AND THE BEES

All living things in the world ultimately die. Therefore it is imperative, from nature's perspective, that all living things replace themselves if the natural world is to continue to exist. This includes the birds and bees, plants and trees, cats and dogs, and yes, human beings. This replacement process is referred to as sexual reproduction.

Humans, the most developed mammal in the natural world, have a complicated reproductive cycle. First, the female has to mature sexually, which occurs usually some time after age twelve, when she is able to release mature eggs on a monthly basis. In order for her to be mature from a reproductive point of view, she needs to have her hormones released in a cyclical fashion. In the first part of her monthly cycle, estrogen is secreted, and then progesterone is added in the second half of the cycle. These two hormones, working together, prepare the lining of her uterus, the endometrium, to be able to nourish and support a fertilized egg. The maturation process in the female is considered complete when this occurs. It is best recognized when the female finally develops regular, predictable blood flow from her uterus through the vagina and out to the exterior. This external bleeding is normally called "a period" and is referred to as the menstrual cycle.

Sex

In order for a mature girl to become pregnant, her vagina, or occasionally only her vulva, needs to be exposed to sperm from a male partner at the time she releases an egg. This release or "ovulation" is usually during the middle of her monthly cycle. This "coming together" of the female with the male is called sexual intercourse. Intercourse becomes possible when the male is sexually stimulated, has an erection, and the firm penis can then enter the vagina through the hymen and vulva. As the result of being enclosed in the vagina, and the accompanying friction of movement, the male releases sperm from the penis, usually into the top of the vagina near the neck of the uterus, which is called the cervix. The release of sperm is called ejaculation, and the male experiences an orgasm during this release. The feeling of an orgasm is related to rhythmical contractions of his pelvic muscles and male organs. This experience is pleasurable for him.

Females do not need to have an orgasm themselves to get pregnant. However, over time, penetration of the penis into the vagina normally becomes pleasurable for her as well. Once comfortable, she begins to experience orgasms. Orgasms, achieved with a committed partner in a secure and private place, become a more regular feature during intercourse.

Strange as the sex act may seem, putting a penis into a vagina (sexual intercourse), is an adult activity that is for many people enjoyed over a lifetime. Not only is sexual intercourse nature's answer for having children, it also provides pleasure for the couple in the most intimate and caring of moments. It becomes one of the most important aspects of a true loving relationship. In an ideal world, this sexual bond between a man and woman is unbroken, and over time, hopefully, a life-long commitment forms.

All of this physical, hormonal, and deep emotional stuff can be a bit overwhelming for an emerging adult, causing further doubts and concerns about this part of growing up. So let us deal with that.

Chapter Seven

SEXUAL ISSUES

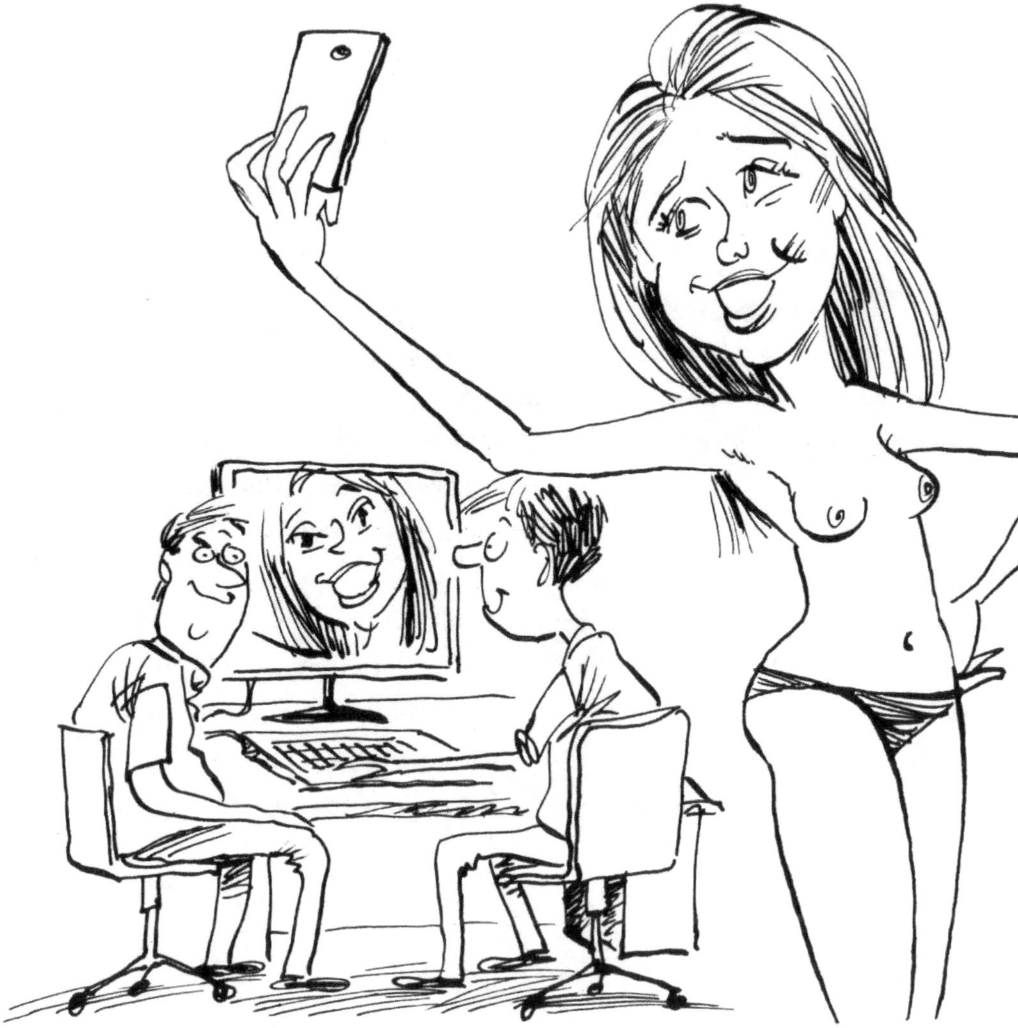

EARLY HUMAN SEXUALITY

The most critical aspect of life is nature's ability to reproduce itself. Humans are no exception. Built into all of us is the ability to replace ourselves, and directing this most critical need is our own sexuality and sex drive. Prior to puberty and before the onset of sex hormone production, children appreciate that they are either male or female. They have no urge to express themselves in a physical, sexual sense. However, after puberty, and for most of one's remaining life, each individual has sexual feelings and a sex drive. We feel compelled to understand and appreciate these sexual urges, but need to be able to control and manage them. Developing a healthy sexual self is part of the maturation process, as is respecting and following cultural rules.

It is during these early pubescent and adolescent years that a healthy individual sexuality should become ingrained. Unfortunately, this does not always occur for everyone, as there are many pitfalls to trap the young person; some have severe and lifelong consequences. It is these feelings that we must focus on, try to understand, and ultimately control.

SEXUAL ABUSE

The touching of a child's sexual organs, namely the vulva, vagina, breasts, or penis, by an adult, is, by law, sexual abuse. It is also sexual abuse if there is a significant age difference between a child and an older teenager (the abuser). Sexual abuse does not have to be forced, painful, or involve penetration; it includes any behaviour, such as looking at or showing sexual organs to a child, which satisfies the adult's fantasy or sexual needs. This behaviour, by a person much older than the child, is difficult to understand. Sadly, it occurs far too often and happens, in most circumstances, with individuals whom the child knows, such as a stepfather, family member, friend of the family, babysitter, etc. Rarely are strangers involved.

Girls are most at risk, but boys can also be victims. Most parents are aware of the possibility for sexual abuse. They advise their children that "no one is to touch your private parts," and if someone tries to, "say no and tell me." Sexual abuse of a child is against the law, and if not handled well, has both short and long-term consequences. The adult involved faces the full force of the law, which requires jail time if convicted. The adult abuser is marked for life as a childhood sexual predator. This individual requires counselling, and in many circumstances, life-long supervision. The abused child also needs support and counselling, but fortunately, with professional help, she or he can recover, though some victims may always be troubled by what happened.

PORNOGRAPHY AND CHILDREN

Pornography is printed or visual material, published in books, magazines, photographs, films or pictures to view on the Internet, that depict sexual images or behaviour. Such pornography is designed to stimulate and arouse sexual interest. Pornography is legal: some adults use it extensively for their own sexual curiosity and gratification. Tragically, it is all too accessible to young people. Far too much of this material focuses on minors and young people. It is often obscene, demeaning, violent, and totally inappropriate, especially for young minds trying to come to terms with their own developing sexuality. The wrong impression is portrayed and may have disturbing consequences. A healthy, normal sexuality is not the focus of much of pornography: thus a warped view of sex is learned. The Internet is full of images that the adolescent often wants to view and explore. Parents, schools, and society must be aware of how damaging it can be. Easy access to the Internet for young developing minds is a mixed blessing. It has many great benefits for the teenager, but its darker side needs to be addressed and somehow controlled.

SEXTING

Sexting is the act of sending and receiving sexually explicit messages, most commonly between mobile phones. Today, people in general, and teenagers in particular, are comfortable texting or sending emails that have sexual overtones, explicit language, or photographs. Somehow people forget that once they press "Send", their message may be out there forever. Over the coming days, weeks, months, and even years, what they have texted or posted as pictures can still be found. These can be used by others to torment them and may haunt them for some time. How we feel today is often much different from how we will feel tomorrow or next month, so we all need to be cautious about what we say, write, text, or do, to avoid ever having to regret our careless actions. Your sexting can be held against you.

Most importantly, never get involved with anyone you don't know. This is especially true for contacts in cyberspace. Tragically, some teenagers have attempted or actually committed suicide over careless relationships developed on the Internet. A good rule is never to do, say, write online, or text anything that you wouldn't want your family to know. Before expressing yourself online, think long and hard!

Sexual Issues

EARLY SEXUAL EXPERIMENTATION

Part of being an adolescent and teenager is having curiosity to learn more and more. One's sexuality is no exception. As mentioned, our adult culture is full of sexual images and it's normal for young people to want to be part of all that. Our personal sexuality is an expression of our interests, preferences, and orientation. No thoughtful person, including your parents, would want it any other way. This stage in your life is the normal and appropriate time to mature sexually.

Early adolescents may begin to experiment with their sexuality. It is normal to have sensual thoughts and fantasies and to masturbate, particularly for young boys. It is not unusual for both sexes to experiment with homosexual and heterosexual partners. This does not mean it will be a lifelong preference. During these early years, powerful romantic and sexual feelings capture the imagination.

In later years, sexual orientation is usually established; "first loves" come center stage. With increasing age, sexual intercourse becomes a real possibility, but before that, a step-by-step progression occurs; from the intimacy of dating, to fondling, to petting, and perhaps even to oral and anal sex before proceeding to vaginal intercourse.

The problem is that even though their minds and bodies are driven to satisfy their sexual feelings, teenagers in advanced societies are not emotionally, intellectually, or financially prepared for the consequences of unprotected sexual activity. What teenager wants to have a baby and take on the responsibility of being a mother or father? The answer is that few teenagers, if they are smart and realistic, think it appropriate. Certainly, most parents don't want their daughter or son to have to deal with a pregnancy at such an early age, and stemming from a relationship that rarely stands the test of time.

Chapter Eight

THE CANDY GENERATION

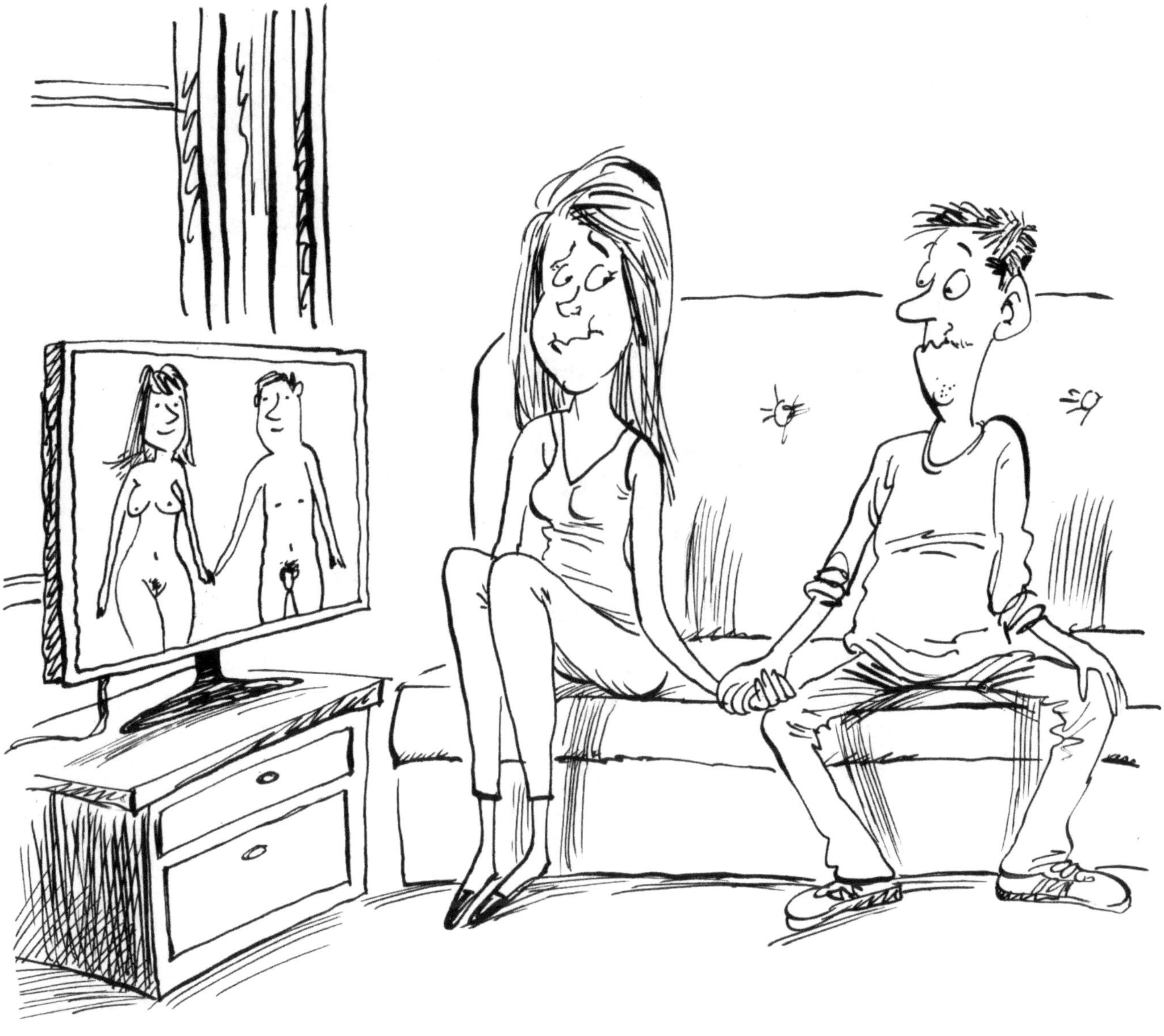

CULTURAL CHALLENGES

As they mature through adolescence toward young adulthood, both sexes are faced with the effects of powerful sex hormones. These hormones influence their brains and bodies to think sexually and want to act differently. In earlier times and in primitive cultures, when lives were much shorter, early reproduction was essential to maintain the continuing life of the species. Adolescent sexual behaviour, including intercourse and having children as teenagers, was normal.

Today in our modern, sophisticated society, having a child in the teenage years can be catastrophic for the pregnant teen, as well as her male partner, their parents, wider families, and society as a whole. More is expected today of young adults than reproducing. There is a need for years of education, more mental maturity to meet the challenges of today's world, and significant financial resources to support themselves before they can ever truly become independent enough to support a child.

Unprotected sex occurs when the couple isn't using any protection or medication to stop ovulation, i.e. oral contraception or a condom (a covering specifically for the penis) or uses it improperly. Lack of protection often leads to an unwanted pregnancy or an infection.

Sadly, our society has not been very helpful in discussing, advising, educating, or supporting young people to delay sexual gratification. Fortunately, there are numerous ways to protect girls from becoming pregnant or infected, but even these are used inconsistently.

Our culture is inundated with sexual images: in advertising products, in print, on television, and online with videos, movies, and pornographic sites. It is unrealistic to expect young people to be immersed in a sexual culture without wanting to experience what all the fuss is about. Sex is "candy" to the adolescent, and too many young people who are tempted then have to live with the consequences. Our culture is at fault, but there appears there is no turning back to earlier, more innocent times.

Early sexual exposure is usually an unplanned or impulsive act, so that often the young female is not physically or mentally prepared for the consequences. "It just happened," or "I wasn't thinking," is the usual response when confronted with nature's reality: a pregnancy!

SEX DRIVE

MALE

Biologically, the male is programmed to have sex when mature. He produces androgens both from his testicles and adrenal glands, and these hormones affect his sexual desire and behaviour. He needs to acknowledge and understand his feelings. Ideally, this insight is learned best from his parents or from other trusted community educators. Unfortunately, too often, his knowledge is learned on the street, on the Internet, or from his peers, and it is spotty information at best—or totally inadequate (even false) at worst.

Learning to accept how he feels and the need to control his impulses and actions are critical to his functioning responsibly as a maturing individual. This is not always possible. Some boys can be aggressive or thoughtless and may often force themselves on the other sex for their own gratification. In certain circumstances it may even become violent. Needless to say, this behaviour is unacceptable. Society has laws to protect those who are hurt by any unwanted sexual acts, and the law can harshly punish those committing them.

FEMALE

Female sexuality is different from that of boys. Young girls like to feel attractive, desirable, cared for and loved. They like to be held, caressed, and fondled, but are not initially as driven as boys to have sexual intercourse. For most females there is nothing liberating about a heartless, uncommitted sexual partner. Women's sexual behaviour can be full of risks. Certainly, an unwanted pregnancy is the most undesirable consequence. Having a child, with all that it entails, or having a termination of the pregnancy (an abortion), are not the consequences envisaged from just "playing around".

Intercourse also presents the risk of infection. Some are quite serious, such as gonorrhea, herpes, and AIDS, all of which have lifelong negative consequences.

Prior to the development of the oral contraceptive, young girls were taught by their parents and culture to abstain from sex before marriage. Women's sexuality was denied, repressed, and even punished. However, once a pregnancy could be prevented, women in advanced societies felt liberated from that natural reality and fear.

This led to a sexual revolution; women wanted the liberty to be less sexually inhibited, to be equal to men, and to have the same sexual options. This led to many young females having numerous sexual experiences and multiple partners. It was not too long before women found out that these new freedoms, experiences, and pleasures were often not as gratifying as they had thought they would be. Casual sex, with few or no real feelings involved, could be degrading. It seems that the sexual revolution has taught us that sexual behaviour is deeply gender-specific. Today, adolescents and other more mature women who are free with their bodies may feel used, abused, and cheap, and might appear so to others as well.

Nature has instilled in us a strong biological drive to reproduce, and our culture promotes sex in all its aspects, so that it takes tremendous will power to say "NO!"

Adult sexual behaviour involving intercourse during adolescence is not always all that it is cracked up to be! This "candy" can have a profound, unpleasant aftertaste.

Chapter Nine

UNWANTED PREGNANCY

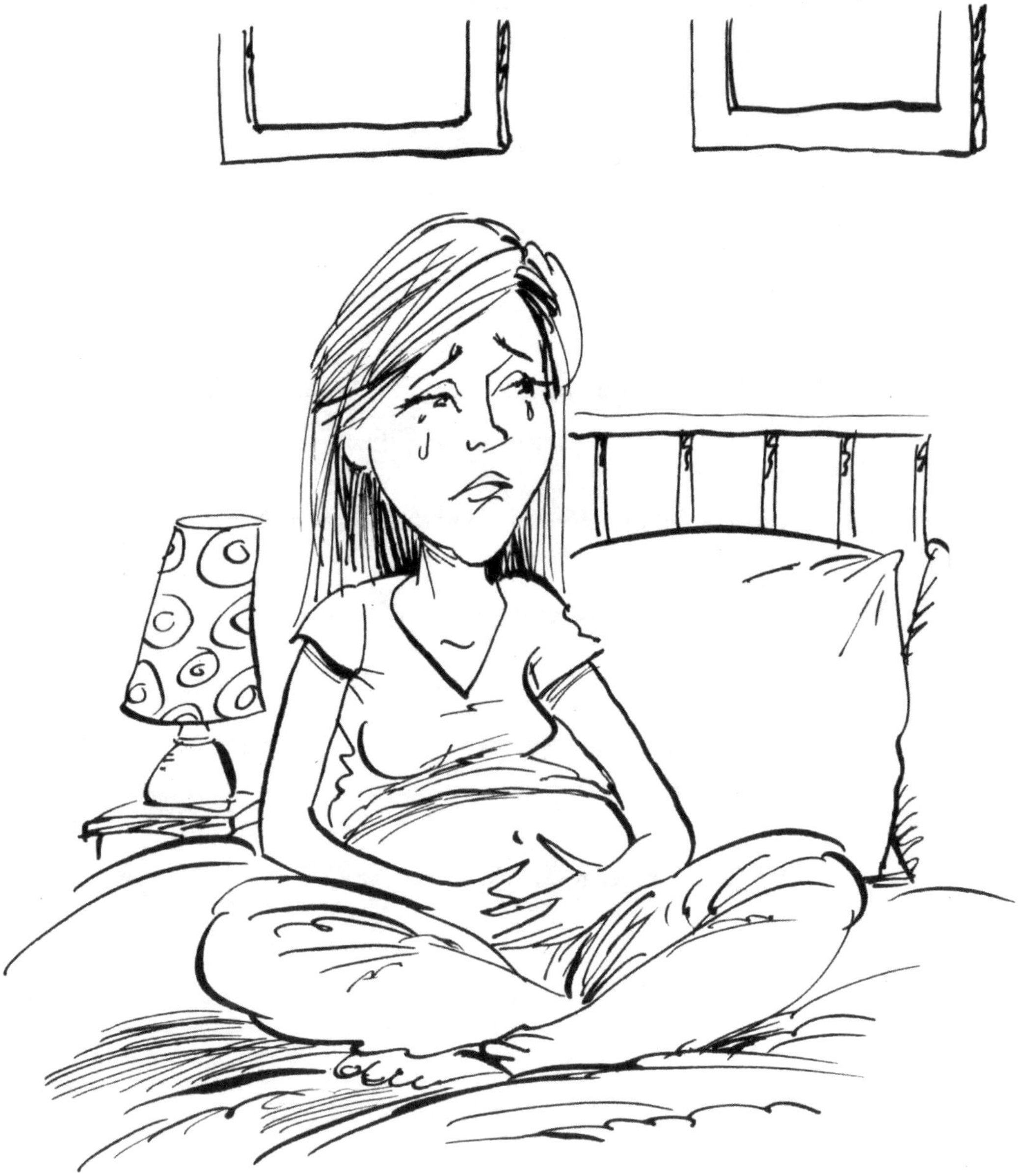

STARTLING FACTS

1) A sexually active teenager who doesn't use contraception has a 90% chance of becoming pregnant in one year.

2) Half of all mothers on welfare had their first child as a teenager.

3) Two-thirds of families begun by young, unmarried mothers end up poor.

4) Eight out of ten of the males responsible for the pregnancy don't marry the mother.

5) Less than 2% of teenage mothers ever earn a university degree.

TEENAGE MOM

Ultimately, whether to have an abortion or a child has to be the pregnant teenager's decision. Young women who feel optimistic about their futures usually want more education and a career, so if they get pregnant, they often demand an abortion in order to get on with their lives. Teenagers who are discouraged about school, their lives, and future prospects, are generally more inclined to accept the pregnancy.

Once the decision is made to have the child, it is imperative that the pregnant teenager be cared for medically and psychologically, and for the pregnancy to be monitored routinely by her physician or caregiver. Since the diagnosis of pregnancy is often delayed and then denied, a lot of the normal prenatal assessment time and care have been missed. Catch-up is required by the caregiver to make sure that the pregnancy itself can be as healthy as possible.

It is important to note that nature has already designed our species, the human, to have the healthiest pregnancies in the earliest reproductive years. These first pregnancies as teenagers almost invariably have very good health-related outcomes for both mother and child, so there is nothing to be alarmed about from that perspective. Psychologically though, it can be difficult—even life altering—if the mother decides to keep and raise the child herself, often as a single parent, with minimal physical, emotional or financial support.

After the birth of the baby, if the decision is to put the child up for adoption, the newborn will be a real gift and blessing for an infertile couple. Their dreams will have come true, and the child will invariably enjoy an environment of protection, true love, and all the benefits of being treasured by the adopting couple and their extended families.

On a serious note, some teenagers fall out with their parents because of their pregnancy. Not all parents rise to the occasion with "unconditional love". Family stress and possibly a family breakup over a teenage pregnancy are not uncommon. Ideally, all of this should be preventable. With understanding, proper information, a strong family and a supportive society, teenage pregnancies can be managed and lives put back together.

TEENAGE ABORTION

In all societies, the birth of a healthy, wanted child is to be celebrated. However, in today's world and in most advanced countries, an unwanted pregnancy becomes a contentious issue. All involved have to come to terms with what is the new reality and face the difficult choice of having the baby or ending the pregnancy. These two options can be exceedingly difficult, especially for an overwhelmed and stressed young teenager.

After initial denial, the easiest option for the young female is to reject the pregnancy and request to have an abortion. Impulsive decisions are not always the best, so the young, pregnant teenager should have an opportunity to fully discuss her situation with her male partner, the family, and wisely, with an independent professional counsellor. The decision to terminate a pregnancy often has many lifelong consequences for women, with some forever regretting their lost pregnancy.

Before finally making up her mind to have an abortion, the pregnant teenager should look carefully at both scenarios, so that she will know she has made the best decision at the time, and to minimize and accept any concerns or regrets that may arise later in life.

Fortunately, in most developed countries, termination of pregnancy before twenty weeks is legal and is performed by qualified doctors in reputable clinics or hospitals. It is important to know that the earlier the diagnosis of an unwanted pregnancy is made, the easier and safer it is to do. Early on, receiving specialized medication will cause the small growing fetus to die and be expelled from the uterus a few days later. This method requires no surgical intervention. Unfortunately (from a medical perspective), teenagers may hide their pregnancy out of fear and shame, so that when the pregnancy becomes obvious, the growing fetus has become larger and more mature, and surgically removing it comes with more significant risks and may have more consequences. From a risk point of view, the earlier the diagnosis and decision to terminate are made, the better for all concerned.

There are still some areas of the world where abortions are illegal, and some societies and religions ban the procedure outright. In these circumstances, women who are determined to terminate their pregnancy have often been forced to have illegal abortions by unqualified persons, often performed in unsuitable circumstances. This scenario can end poorly, with an incomplete abortion, excessive bleeding and/or infection. This unacceptable result often necessitates further surgery. In some circumstances, because of complications, some women may be unable to have children at a future date. Occasionally, with poor care, women have died from serious complications.

Chapter Ten

ALTERNATE SEXUAL BEHAVIOURS

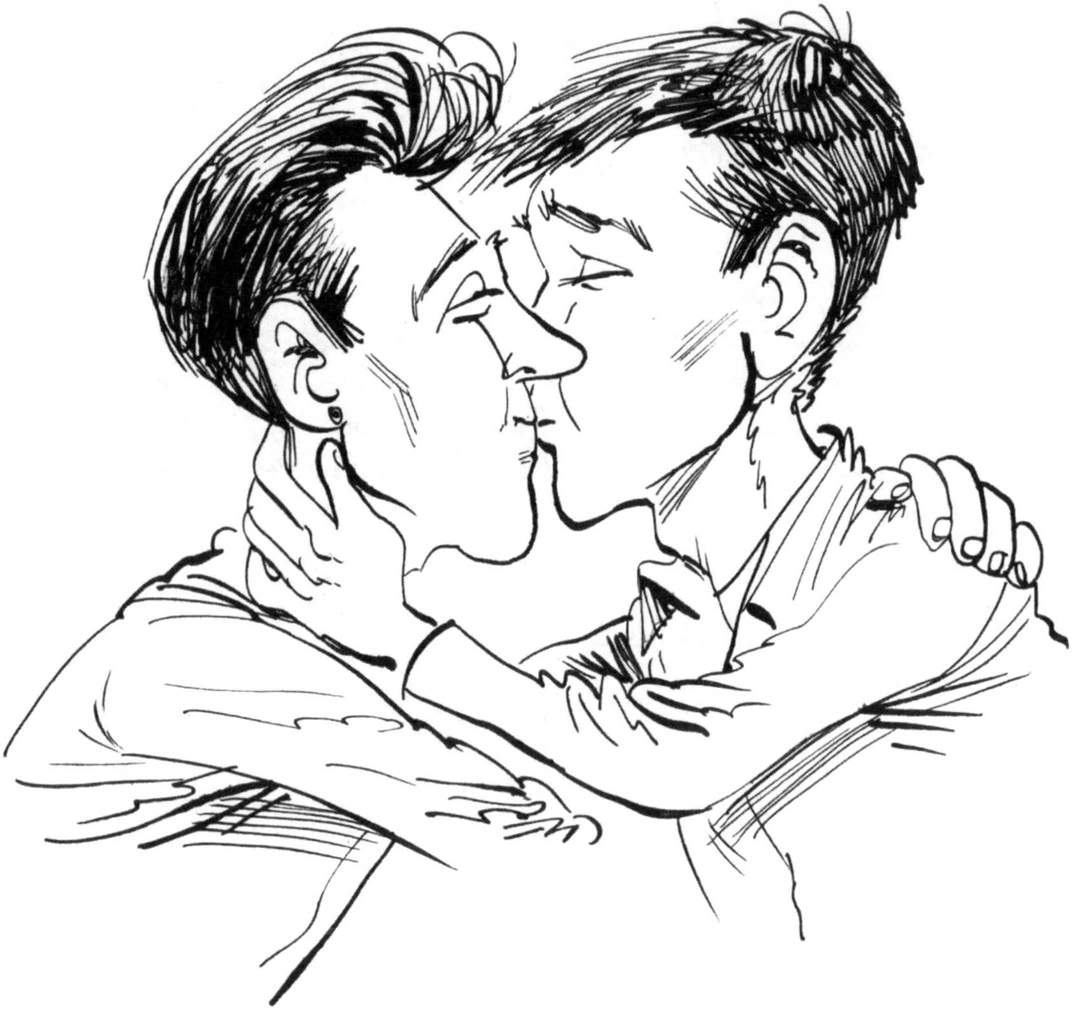

HOMOSEXUALITY

Certain mature people are not driven by traditional male-female (straight/ heterosexual) sexual desire. As young teenagers, it is not uncommon to fantasize about sex, have sexual feelings and engage in early experimentation, which sometimes involves the same sex. Sexual attraction to those of the same sex can be quite confusing and alarming. In the adolescent social world, being gay (male-male) or lesbian (female-female) can have high social costs. These young adolescents may be teased, ostracized and persecuted.

Confusion can reign when one transitions from an asexual child to first experimenting in same-sex relationships. Ultimately, over time, most individuals develop strong heterosexual feelings and act accordingly. However, a percentage are not interested in the opposite sex as sexual partners, but are sexually attracted to those of the same sex.

Sexual drive is a force to be recognized, understood, and managed. The consequences of one's choices can be difficult, not only in a social context but also in health-related issues. This we learned from the earlier epidemics of AIDS, which were initially encountered in the homosexual community. Fortunately, in sophisticated medical societies, AIDS is no longer a death sentence for the individual infected, but it does remain a lifelong problem requiring continual medical management.

Alternate Sexual Behaviours

With increasing acceptance, gay and lesbian individuals no longer have to hide their sexual orientation from the wider community, as they did in the past. They are more visible in our culture, prominent in the media, and usually well respected in their fields of endeavour. Nonetheless, in spite of our more open and accepting society, it is not easy to be different, especially in certain cultures and traditional religious families. It is important to recognize that we are all different, and that each person should be respected as a unique individual. We each choose and lead our own lives. It is not for us to judge, but to allow others to be true to themselves. Does it really matter whom we love? Our sexuality is our own, and should be allowed to be lived in private.

LGBTQ COMMUNITY

LGBTQ is a spoken and written term that refers to those whose sexual orientation differs from the heterosexual norm.

> L: Lesbian (Female-Female sexual attraction)
>
> G: Gay (Male-Male sexual attraction)
>
> B: Bisexual (Sexual attraction to both male and female)
>
> T: Transsexual (Feels they belong to the opposite sex)
>
> Q: Queer (Questioning one's own sexuality)

In essence, a small portion of adults actually deviates from the biological norm of heterosexuality (male–female), i.e. straight. Although a minority of adults has other feelings and impulses, these people need to be respected and valued as they are.

OF REAL CONCERN

ABUSIVE SEX

Parents want their children to grow up with healthy sexual attitudes (and preferably in a heterosexual relationship, because life will likely be less challenging for all concerned). That vision, which is ideal for the maturing adolescent, can be, but often is not what teenagers see in their sexualized society. Commercials, television dramas, and the ever-pervasive Internet, with its sexual content and pornography, too often display sex violently, degradingly, or depicted with male dominance. If, at the same time, teenagers see some of this behaviour at home or in their culture, they get terribly mixed messages.

The best way for everyone to develop a healthy sexuality is to recognize that although abusive sex exists as a very disturbing fact of life, it is entirely inappropriate. Parents and our wider society must address the issue openly, educating teenagers about this possibility, so that they are aware of the negative aspects that can coexist in sexual relationships. The best way to counteract degrading sexual behaviour is to observe people in respectful, loving relationships as the ultimate role models. To growing and maturing adolescents, nothing is more important to help them develop their own positive sexuality.

TEENAGE PROSTITUTION

Tragically, and usually through no fault of their own, some teenagers feel lonely, become isolated from family and friends, and lack any hope for the future. Their situation sometimes involves a family break-up, poverty, sexual abuse, and often, poor life choices. One of these choices may be teenage prostitution, which refers to an individual paying, either with money or gifts, for sexual acts from an adolescent before the age of legal consent. Child prostitution is illegal. There are two main forms it can take.

The first type is "Survival Sex". This occurs when the teenager, often living alone, engages in sexual acts as a necessary means to survive. Providing sex to another for money is often done to pay for a place to live, to provide clothing, or to obtain food or drugs. This transaction is usually between the teenager and her contact; there is no middle person involved. The second type is "Commercial Sex". Many of these cases see vulnerable teenagers victimized and exploited by others, such as pimps, madams, or traffickers. They become involved in child pornography or commercial sexual exploitation, often working in bars, clubs, brothels, massage parlours, or on the street.

Before long, these naive and vulnerable teenagers are forced to enter the commercial trade for a quick fix to their lives and for protection. They can earn significant money. Soon, the "prostitute" becomes more deeply ingrained in the culture. She is compelled to join the wider underground of the commercial sex trade, with undertones of drugs and violence. Commercial sex, run by others, is a form of human trafficking. It is a lucrative business for those who exploit the youngest. Sadly, there is a high demand for young people and extremely high profits for the exploiters.

The young people involved are totally unprepared for the devastating consequences of this subculture. It often results in pain, violence, multiple infections, tears to the vulva and vagina, and unwanted pregnancies. It is a form of torture. The psychological trauma is profound. Beyond the depths of despair and self-loathing are anger, insomnia, lack of trust and depression. Ultimately, as they try to escape their previous reality, this new feeling of worthlessness leads to lives consumed by drug use and poverty. Suicide is not uncommon.

Chapter Eleven

SEXUALLY TRANSMITTED DISEASES

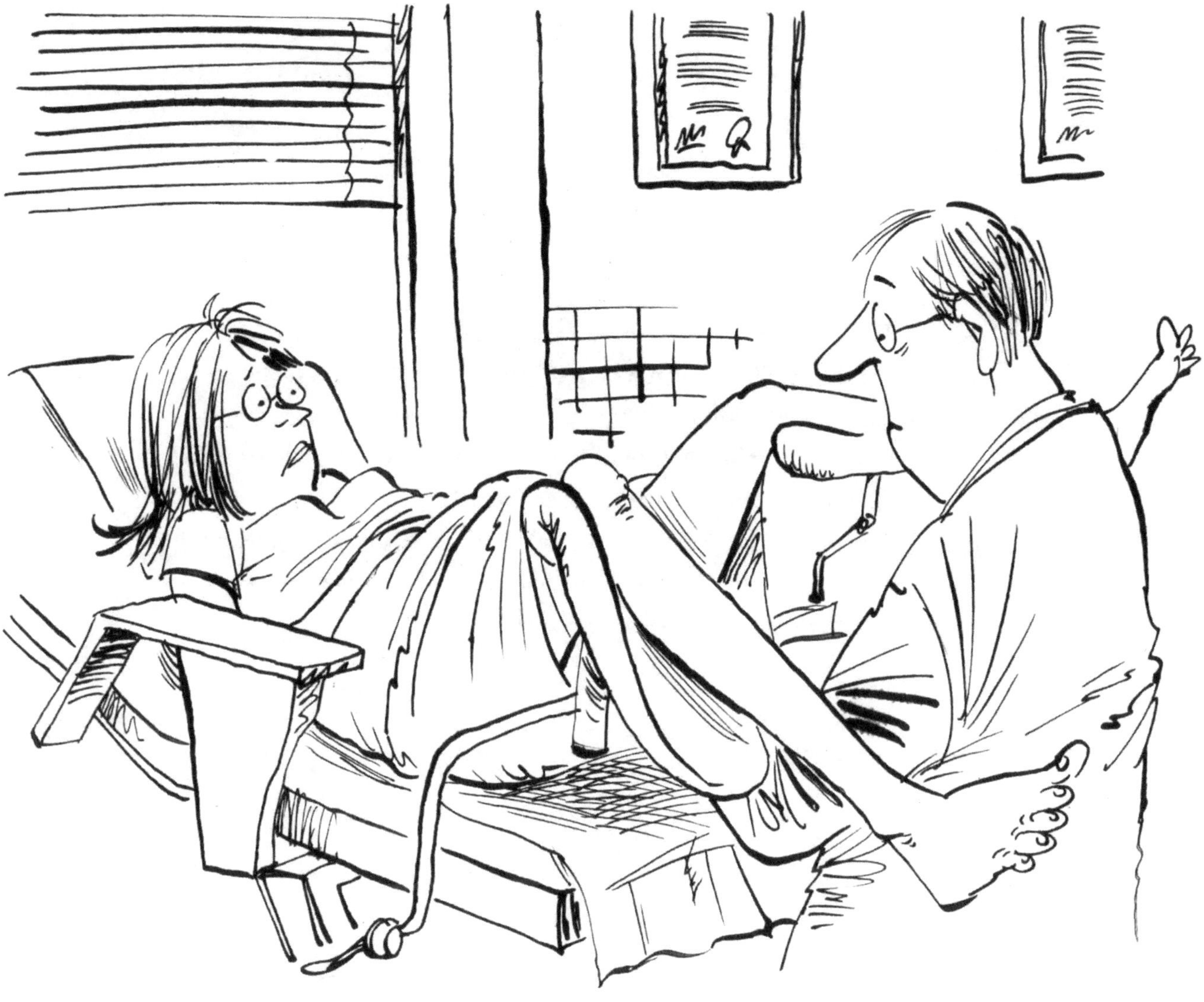

Sexually Transmitted Diseases

Although adolescents make up only 25% of the population, teenagers account for at least 50% of all new sexually transmitted diseases. This is often a result of ignorance about how to protect themselves from acquiring an infection, but also because of their tendency towards more risky behaviour. There is usually a failure of the female to use or insist on a barrier form of contraception, or a refusal of the male to use a condom properly or at all. Multiple partners enhance the risks, as one can never be sure of either partner's previous exposure.

GENITAL HERPES

Genital herpes is a sexually transmitted disease caused by the herpes simplex virus; usually type II, but occasionally type I. It is transmitted by sexual contact and enters the body through the skin or mucous membranes. Often there are no symptoms. In some individuals, though, painful blisters or ulcers are noted in the genital area, accompanied by itching, tingling or a burning sensation. Occasionally patients note flu-like symptoms, with fever, headache, swollen lymph nodes, and general body aches.

Once the virus enters the skin, it travels along nerve pathways, remaining in the body indefinitely. It usually stays inactive or dormant, but on occasion (weeks, months, or even years later) the virus becomes active and travels down the affected nerves, causing symptoms. It can be passed on again with further sexual contact. Condoms can be helpful to prevent its spread, but this is not always guaranteed. There is no cure. Symptoms can be alleviated by treatment with antiviral medications. Some infected people can have many recurrences throughout their lifetime.

HUMAN PAPILLOMA VIRUS (HPV)

Human papilloma virus is the most common of the sexually transmitted diseases. The infection may go away on its own, but more often becomes active, causing genital warts. In some individuals, HPV goes undiagnosed. In these cases, infected people don't recognize that they have been exposed, but nonetheless they harbour the virus for their lifetimes. The virus, which infects the female's genital tract, can be diagnosed by seeing and feeling small bumps on the vulva, in the vagina, or on the cervix. HPV infection is considered precancerous, possibly leading to cancer of the cervix and other areas of the genital tract later in life. There is no cure, but a vaccine is available to prevent infection, and is advised and available for adolescent use.

CHLAMYDIA

The immature cervix of the adolescent is more prone to infection than in adult women. Once a person is infected with chlamydia, the organism is usually passed from partner to partner. In boys, there are symptoms of burning and frequency of urination. In girls, chlamydia causes a discharge or burning sensation, and untreated, the infection can move up the reproductive tract to infect and destroy the fallopian tubes, causing bands of scar tissue (pelvic adhesions) that may prevent a pregnancy in the future (infertility) or result in a tubal or ectopic pregnancy, which may be a life-threatening condition. These complications can be avoided if the infection is diagnosed early enough and appropriately treated with antibiotics.

TRICHOMONAS (TRICH)

A one-celled organism called trichomonas vaginalis causes Trichomonas, the most prevalent, non-viral, sexually transmitted disease. The infection may go unnoticed. It can produce symptoms of vaginal irritation accompanied by a yellowish-green, foul-smelling discharge. Without treatment, the infection can last for months or years. The male partner may also notice an irritation in the urethra (inside the penis), and burning on urination or ejaculation. A few males notice a penile urethral discharge. Treatment is effective. The disease may recur with repeated exposure.

GONORRHEA

Gonorrhea is caused by the bacteria Neisseria gonorrhea, which tends to infect moist, warm areas of the body such as the vagina, the bladder, the urethra, the anus and the throat. Symptoms may occur within a week or shortly after contracting the infection. In the male, the first symptom is burning on urination or increased frequency of urination, often accompanied by a pus-like discharge from the penis. This can be accompanied by swelling and pain in one or both testicles. Women often have minimal or mild symptoms. When symptoms occur, they can include a watery or creamy discharge, pain on urination, heavier periods, pain during intercourse, and lower abdominal discomfort. A fever may also be present.

Complications can be severe. Over time, the infection spreads up through the uterus and fallopian tubes into the pelvis, causing pelvic inflammatory disease (PID). This results in increasing discomfort and potential long-term damage to the internal reproductive organs, which may hamper future reproductive performance. Tubal pregnancies can result from a previous infection or there may be a total inability to get pregnant naturally in the future. In addition, both men and women can have a wide- spread infection, which eventually can lead to a form of arthritis, heart valve damage, and, in a few sufferers, an infection of the brain. Relief of symptoms and prevention of long-term damage are medically available by taking appropriate antibiotics.

SYPHILIS

Syphilis is caused by the bacteria Treponema pallidum. Although less commonly seen today, if it is acquired and untreated, it can have serious long-term consequences. Initially, the sexually transmitted infection presents with a single, firm, painless skin ulcer, but if untreated, leads to a rash and other sores on other exposed areas. Years later, if the infection is ignored or undiagnosed, the patient can suffer from heart and neurological problems. This infection can spread from the mother to her child during pregnancy or after birth. Early treatment will cure it.

HIV-AIDS

HIV stands for Human Immunodeficiency Virus. If untreated, it can lead to AIDS (Acquired Immunodeficiency Syndrome). Undiagnosed and untreated, HIV-AIDS leads to death. Unlike with some viruses, most humans who contract this virus are unable to rid their bodies of it; you have it for life. The result of the acquired infection is an attack on the immune system, which normally protects the body. Once infected, the body can no longer fight off infections, and this weakens the entire body, making it vulnerable to cancer and other diseases.

Most commonly, people transmit HIV through alternate sexual behaviours or intravenous drug use. If a person is infected, all body fluids will contain the virus, so that HIV can be found in blood, semen, and vaginal and rectal fluids, as well as breast milk. Specific testing for the virus is the only way to diagnose the condition. No effective cure exists, but, with proper treatment and good medical care, the disease can be controlled and death prevented, at least for a significant period of time.

Chapter Twelve

RISKY BEHAVIOUR

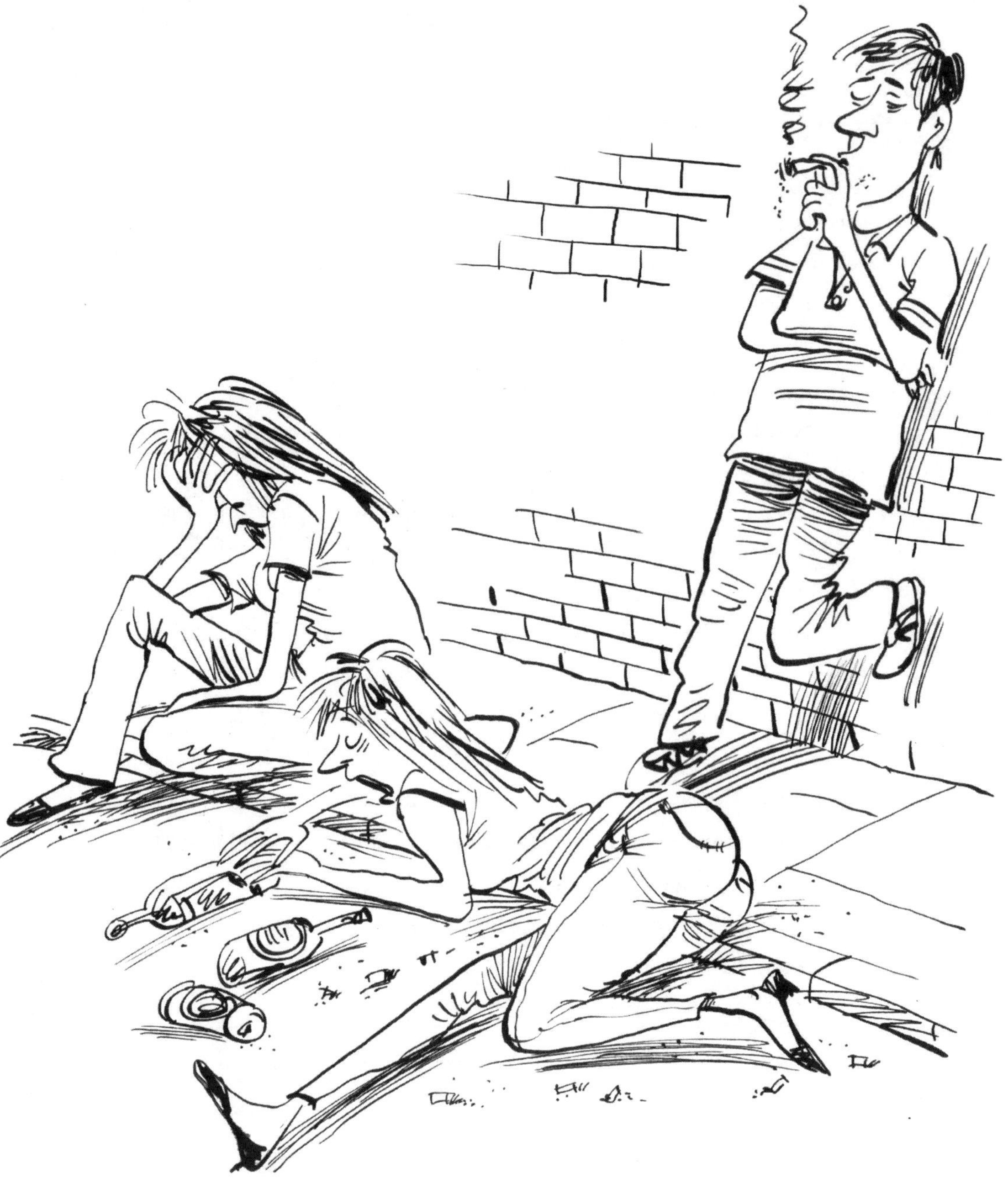

Teenagers see themselves as invulnerable. It is hard to convince themselves otherwise. Up to now, they've probably had it pretty easy, thanks to lots of supervision over the years from family, friends, their schools, and society at large.

Not all risky behaviour is bad. Experience is our best teacher as we learn, gain skills, and develop our own self-esteem. During their adolescent years, teenagers must come to terms with themselves physically, mentally, and emotionally. At the same time, they must begin to develop their own values and moral convictions. They must also take responsibility for both the positive and negative outcomes resulting from their actions. The real concerns arise when a young adult doesn't really understand or know the risks of experimenting with unsafe substances or behaviours.

With thoughtful upbringing and good role models early in life, many adolescents are able to find themselves and sail safely through the troubled waters of growing up. Sometimes, though, teenagers head down side channels, often having to turn around and come back, until ultimately finding themselves. Others, less fortunate, crash on the rocks. The potential for these poor choices needs to be addressed early on—before any serious consequences occur.

SMOKING

Smoking cigarettes used to be very common and acceptable worldwide. The habit was often adopted early, between ages fourteen and eighteen, because smoking made young adults feel grown up, mature, and "sexy". If parents smoke, their children see that as normal behaviour, which they copy by lighting up. Peer pressure is also a big factor, as teenagers want to "fit in", "be cool", and be well liked and part of the "in" crowd. Smoking can also be a defiance statement; the teen wants to be independent by ignoring any advice not to smoke. Because of the well-known health hazards, gone are the days of direct advertising of cigarettes, but more subtle messaging that promotes continued use appears on television, in movies, and on the Internet.

Why is smoking so bad? Smoking becomes addictive due to the nicotine in tobacco, which requires those who smoke to continue to get "their fix". Simply put, smoking always leads to more smoking, and invariably to health problems. Tobacco smoke is an irritant to the mouth, to the tubes connecting the back of the mouth to the lungs (trachea), and to the lungs themselves. This irritation leads ultimately to a chronic cough and increased secretions of mucus in the throat and trachea. The carbon particles found in the smoke always become lodged in the lung itself. Eventually, the normally pink lungs become black with the embedded carbon, and the delicate portions of the lungs that provide us with oxygen break down and stop functioning, leaving the smoker short of breath. Chronic, long-term exposure to smoke, coupled with the chemicals and particles found in the smoke, cause a vast number of people to go on to develop cancer of the lungs and die earlier than they otherwise would. Death from lung cancer can be horrible, as you are continually gasping for air. No, it's not cool to begin to smoke or continue smoking! Smoking means only that you are ill informed, stupid, or don't care for yourself—not a flattering image you want to create!

ALCOHOL

Alcohol in our society is the "drug of choice". It is widely available and aggressively promoted. Most countries have enacted laws that stipulate at what age alcohol can be consumed. For many, early alcohol consumption appears to be part of the growing up experience, and the law is too often ignored. Yet under-age drinking is dangerous, not only for the drinker but also for society as a whole.

When anything is off limits, teenagers want to see why. Everything they hear about the effects of beer, wine, and spirits raises their interest. Peer pressure contributes to the desire. Teens want to be hip, grown up, and with it. The thrill of drinking, with its expectations of pleasure, is just too much temptation. Once they try it, they begin to feel more at ease in certain situations, especially in social ones, where they may be struggling.

Unfortunately, the teen doesn't appreciate the consequences and side effects of alcohol. Alcohol use leads to drowsiness, lack of coordination, and brain suppression. The brain itself becomes impaired, resulting in unpredictable and often crazy behaviour. Often, the drinker doesn't appreciate the side effects until something unforeseen, and sometimes serious, happens.

Alcohol is a potent substance, created when grains, fruits, or vegetables are fermented. Yeast or bacteria alters the sugar content of these natural products, producing alcohol. This chemical reaction is called fermentation. When people drink alcohol, it is quickly absorbed into the bloodstream, circulates to all parts of the body, and most noticeably affects the brain. Alcohol is a depressant, not a stimulant. It alters a person in many ways, affecting body movements, causing dizziness, distorting vision and even one's overall perception of the situation at hand. It can have profound emotional and intellectual effects as well.

In small amounts, alcohol does make people more relaxed, confident, and less anxious. But more alcohol causes confusion, disorientation, incoordination, and slurred speech. Some people become more talkative and overtly friendly, while others become angry and hostile. Reaction times are slowed. Large amounts of alcohol consumed over a short period of time can result in actual poisoning. Vomiting occurs, often violently, followed by drowsiness and sometimes unconsciousness, all the while causing difficulty in breathing. In the most severe situations, convulsions can occur, followed by death.

As mentioned earlier, drinking is against the law before age eighteen in some countries and age twenty-one in others—and for good reasons. Teens who drink too much are more likely to cause trouble for society and its law enforcement officers; vandalism, fighting, and more serious criminal offences can result. Drinking teenagers make very poor choices. Too often, when drunk, they become obnoxious, have unsafe sex resulting in unwanted pregnancies, or acquire one or more sexually transmitted diseases. None of it good!

Alcohol is another form of addiction. Teens who begin early or drink excessively are more likely to develop a problem with alcohol long-term. It appears that genetics may play a role in becoming dependent on alcohol to support one's life. In addition, there are a number of other factors that can influence abusers. These include the teenagers' family environment and stresses they can't handle. Alcohol makes life easier; at least that is what they initially think! Tragically, alcohol use in teenagers is associated with many negative outcomes. Poor performance in school, with unfulfilled potential, often leads to early dropout.

Most importantly, alcohol use and abuse is far too often implicated in motor vehicle accidents. For the majority of drivers between the ages of sixteen and twenty who are killed in car accidents, alcohol consumption is cited as the main cause, or at least a complicating factor. Early alcohol use has been shown to be associated with other later substance abuses, making alcohol an early marker of concern. If the abuse is curbed, it may prevent the possibility of developing other risky behaviours down the road, such as addiction to a more serious drug.

MARIJUANA
(Weed)

Marijuana is derived from the leaves, flowers, and other parts of the hemp plant (Cannabis sativa). The hemp plant has a chemical, Delta-9-Tetrahydrocannabinol (THC), which contains inherently mind-altering properties. Today, marijuana is the most commonly used mind-altering drug, and in many jurisdictions, it is illegal. It is widely available, and teenagers and young adults are its most avid users. It can be smoked in hand-rolled cigarettes known as "joints" or in pipes called "bongs." In addition, it can be mixed into foods such as brownies, cookies, or candies. Marijuana can also be brewed as a tea.

Once smoked or consumed, THC passes from the lungs or the gastrointestinal tract, to the bloodstream, where the chemical attaches to receptors in the brain and other organs. The brain is the most sensitive organ of the body to the active ingredient in marijuana, which causes a "high". The senses are altered and enhanced, i.e. colours are brighter and there is a change in mood and a distortion of time, along with impaired memory. Individuals using the compound can have difficulty with their thought processes, their coordination, and general movements.

Concern arises especially for young people, who have immature and growing brains. Research suggests that early marijuana use in teenagers may decrease the intelligence (IQ) of those using it. The effect may be life-long. Long-term use has been linked to mental illness. Under the influence of THC, the individual may begin seeing things (hallucination), distrust others (paranoia), and have disorganized thinking. In addition, depression, anxiety and suicidal thoughts have been linked to its use.

Heavy users often experience lower life satisfaction, poor physical health, and relationship problems. Poor school performance is common, as is job absenteeism. Users exhibit poor motivation. A higher incidence of car accidents and injuries has been noted. Naturally, there is real concern about driving under the influence, since marijuana appears to at least double the incidence of motor vehicle accidents. At present, the law is ill equipped to instantly and positively identify those under the influence, or to establish a legal limit, as has been done for alcohol. Is any amount too much?

Is marijuana truly addictive? Many users smoke joints frequently and appear dependent on it in their lives, but true addiction, with the inability to stop its use, is rare. Marijuana smoke irritates the respiratory tract, much like smoking cigarettes, resulting in increased production of mucus, chronic coughing, and lung infections. The jury is out on whether it causes lung cancer.

Use of marijuana, like alcohol and tobacco, is of concern. It may demonstrate, in those individuals using it, a tendency towards more risky behaviour. Some may only be attracted occasionally and under peer pressure. They think it's no big deal. Other teenagers who use it frequently may be demonstrating dissatisfaction with their lives and are trying to escape the stresses and burdens they perceive. The worry is that they may, over time, want to try more potent mind-altering substances, which have much more serious consequences.

Chapter Thirteen

DESTRUCTIVE BEHAVIOUR

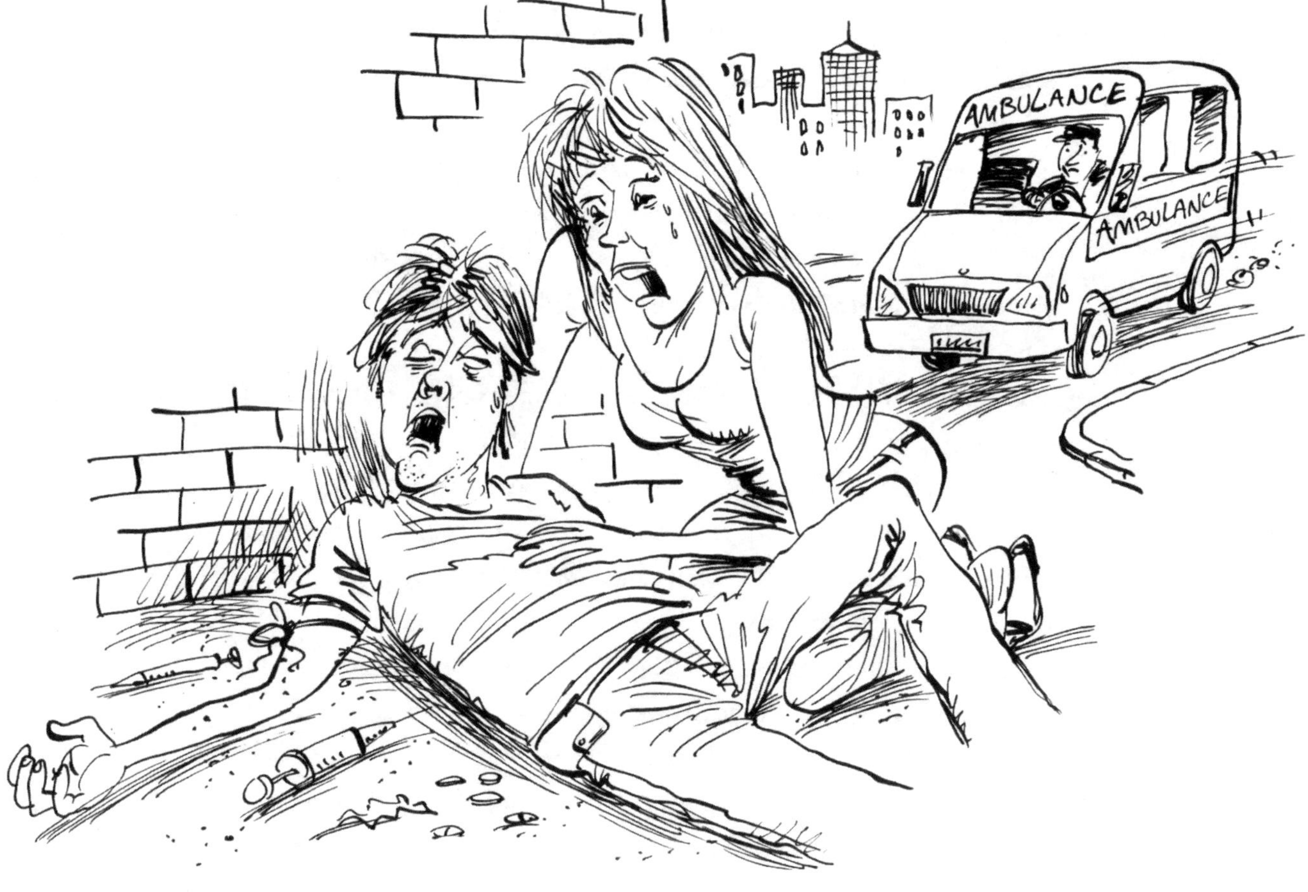
AMBULANCE
AMBULANCE

ILLEGAL DRUG USE

The modern world, and particularly the Western world, must take a great deal of the responsibility for the portion of our youth that is feeling isolated and forgotten. It is not unusual for those passing from childhood to adulthood to feel overwhelmed, inadequate, and unable to cope with the demands of this modern, ever-changing world. If their families, friends, society, or culture fail them, or if it appears that there is little or nothing positive for them, teenagers will look for something—anything—that gives them pleasure and relieves them of the feeling of hopelessness.

In cases of addiction, there can be tremendous peer pressure, along with disinformation, that encourages unhappy and frustrated teenagers to try to escape. Teenagers often feel bored, don't like being alone, and are always looking for excitement or a way to bond with others in similar circumstances. When one is angry or aggressive, it is not unusual to rebel from society's norms.

Substance abuse, especially illegal drug use, may provide instant gratification; drugs work quickly, the individual feels better, and, in the short-term, they provide the illusion of happiness. If the teenager lacks confidence, drug use alleviates social anxiety, loosens inhibitions, and converts a shy individual into a more outgoing one. It's unfortunate that a great deal of misinformation is gleaned from those selling or already using the drugs.

Tragically, some teenagers move beyond tobacco, alcohol, or marijuana. Although those substances can have some repercussions, they are usually controllable. Once teenagers begin to use hard drugs, however, it becomes a whole other problem; these drugs are truly addictive and dangerous. There are an enormous number and prevalence of drug choices available to uneducated and vulnerable young people. Hard drug use is a recipe for disaster, not only for individual teenagers, but also for their families and society. It is these highly potent, thoroughly addictive chemicals that can be the most destructive forces on the teenager. Once addicted, these poor, hungry, "down and out" young people are forced from their homes; often left with no choice but to live on the street. A life of crime is usually required to support the ever-increasing costs of the habit before the "drug addict" eventually develops chronic health problems. Over time, he/she may die of infection, malnutrition, an overdose, or even resort to suicide.

COCAINE
(Crack, Coke, Blow, Rock, Snow)

Coca leaves have been chewed and ingested for thousands of years, initially for medical reasons. Chemicals in the coca leaf affect the central nervous system, releasing dopamine within the brain, causing a "high". Over time, the brain can't release and recycle dopamine naturally, so an individual then requires more and more of the drug to feel "normal" and maintain a sense of pleasure. After a person injects or snorts cocaine, it acts instantly. A "high" or euphoria occurs and increased energy is noted, making the user feel more mentally alert, at least for a short period of time. When more and more drug is required to attain this feeling, the individual becomes truly addicted. In addition, there are associated physical changes, with an increased heart rate and blood pressure.

When the drug wears off, the individual often feels restless and anxious, and may begin to panic, behaving erratically and sometimes violently. Even after one dose, heart attacks and strokes may occur. If too much of the drug is taken, seizures, coma, and death may follow. Long-term, repeated use of the drug leads to severe addiction, with all its consequences. Because ever more drugs have to be paid for, criminal behaviour frequently ensues.

OPIOIDS
(Heroin, Morphine, Oxycodone, Fentanyl, Codeine)

Opioids are medicines that, when used appropriately, relieve pain. These compounds act by attaching to receptors in the brain to reduce suffering. Normal side effects of these drugs are drowsiness, confusion, nausea, and perhaps slower respiration. However, some people experience pleasurable sensations, which they find irresistible. The positive effect is short-term—followed by severe withdrawal symptoms of restlessness, muscle pain, insomnia, diarrhea, and vomiting. More of the drug is consumed just to feel better again, and over time, higher and higher doses are required just to feel normal.

STIMULANTS
(Crystal Meth, Speed)

Crystal meth, like cocaine, heroin, and the other drugs mentioned in this chapter, is an illegal drug. It is a highly addictive stimulant that's taken through the nose (snorting), by smoking it, or by injection. It immediately causes a false sense of happiness and confidence that lasts for up to eight hours. After that time, fatigue, depression, and disturbed sleep occur. The chemical is itself a poison, which eventually destroys the brain and results in memory loss, aggressiveness, psychotic behaviour, and seizures.

ECSTASY
(MDMA, Molly)

Ecstasy is a synthetic drug that alters both mood and perception. It is a stimulant, but also a hallucinogen, causing the release of norepinephrine, serotonin, and dopamine from the brain. This results in euphoria, increased energy, increased heart rate, and interestingly, elevated mood and emotional closeness. Because of these effects, it is trendy for all-night parties known as "raves". It can be taken in tablet form or as a powder by snorting it. As with all of these compounds, there are many side effects, including nausea, blurred vision, chills, sweats, muscle cramps, anxiety, and memory loss.

HALLUCINOGENS
(LSD, Ketamine, Dextromethorthan, Mescaline, Etc.)

Hallucinogens are a diverse group of chemicals that alter perception, thoughts, and feelings. They can be found in some plants, most notably from the Amazon, like cacti and mushrooms, or they can be man-made. For centuries, some of them have been used for religious rituals. They work by acting through the chemical serotonin to disrupt communication within the brain. The effect begins within thirty to sixty minutes and can last up to twelve hours. Users refer to their experience as a "trip", and an unpleasant one is called a "bad trip."

For the user, there are changes in one's sense of time, intensified feelings, and heightened sensory experiences. These compounds can have undesirable side effects such as loss of appetite, dry mouth, uncoordinated movements, sweating, and panic attacks. In addition, there can be long-term effects such as memory loss, weight loss, depression, and suicidal thoughts. Some users have a series of continuing mental problems, with disorganized thinking, paranoia, mood changes, and visual disturbances. Flashbacks are also troubling.

INHALANTS
(Chemicals and Household Products)

There are many common household products that can, when sniffed, affect the brain. People using them are usually trying to escape from their sad realities. Often young teens find pleasure from the vapours of cleaning fluids, glue, paint, nail polish remover, gasoline, or aerosol sprays. They are all poisons that negatively affect the brain. Over time, they can have profound effects on thinking, speaking, and even walking.

SUICIDE ATTEMPTS

Discussing premature death is never easy, yet it's important if we are to try to understand some adolescents' behaviour. Fortunately, killing oneself (suicide) is extremely rare in childhood, but the incidence increases greatly during adolescent years. In fact, it is one of the most common causes of death for youngsters between the ages of fifteen and nineteen. Girls think about and attempt suicide more often than boys; however, actual death occurs more for boys than for girls, as they tend to use more lethal methods (guns, motor vehicle crashes, jumping from heights).

Suicide by a young person is the result of an overwhelming feeling of hopelessness and helplessness. The teenager is trying to escape from a situation that seems impossible to deal with, such as rejection, shame, or guilt. The teen may also be a victim of circumstances (online bullying, prostitution), and feel the only way to deal with it is to end his/her life. Addiction to illegal drugs, too, often results in suicide.

Young people contemplating suicide feel unwanted, unloved, and may believe they are a burden to their family or friends. Suicide attempts can result from many experiences: rejection by peers, bullying, fear of sexual orientation, or in the wake of sexual abuse. Other issues, such as domestic abuse, parental divorce, or just plain stress from pressure at school can trigger a suicide attempt. Too often the student or his/her family may have unrealistically high expectations. Sometimes, the student is a perfectionist and not willing to fail.

A suicide attempt is rarely the symptom of a desire to die; rather, it is an attempt to escape from a perceived reality. Less commonly, the attempt is related to a long-term mental disorder rather than as a result of a current depression.

No situation in life, no matter how it seems at the time, is worth ending one's own life. There is no question that at times life can seem—and truly be—difficult for many of us. When we are children, our family, friends, and schools provide a shield from many of life's difficulties, but once we gain more freedom and independence, the real world can be much more challenging, especially emotionally.

For some troubled young adults, lines of open communication are not easily accessible, so depressed teens often lack the support they need to confide in someone early on. Even if it is by going online, crying out is important to reach the necessary help. For all of us, it is an obligation to address and try to prevent suicide. For those just starting out, thoughts of suicide can be a real tragedy. Medical, psychological, and emotional support are available in most communities, so it is important for those who suffer from severe depression to know where to turn in a crisis.

First, young people with suicidal thoughts need to contact someone whom they trust, rather than withdrawing from others to suffer alone.

That trusted person might be your parents, a best friend, a neighbour, a teacher at school, a relative, or it could be your doctor or minister. Whoever you contact will, in turn, give you as much support as they can, and connect you with an appropriate care provider, be it a hospital or a service specifically funded to meet your needs. Many communities have a Suicide Crisis Line, which can be found on the Internet.

Chapter Fourteen

LIFESTYLE CHOICES

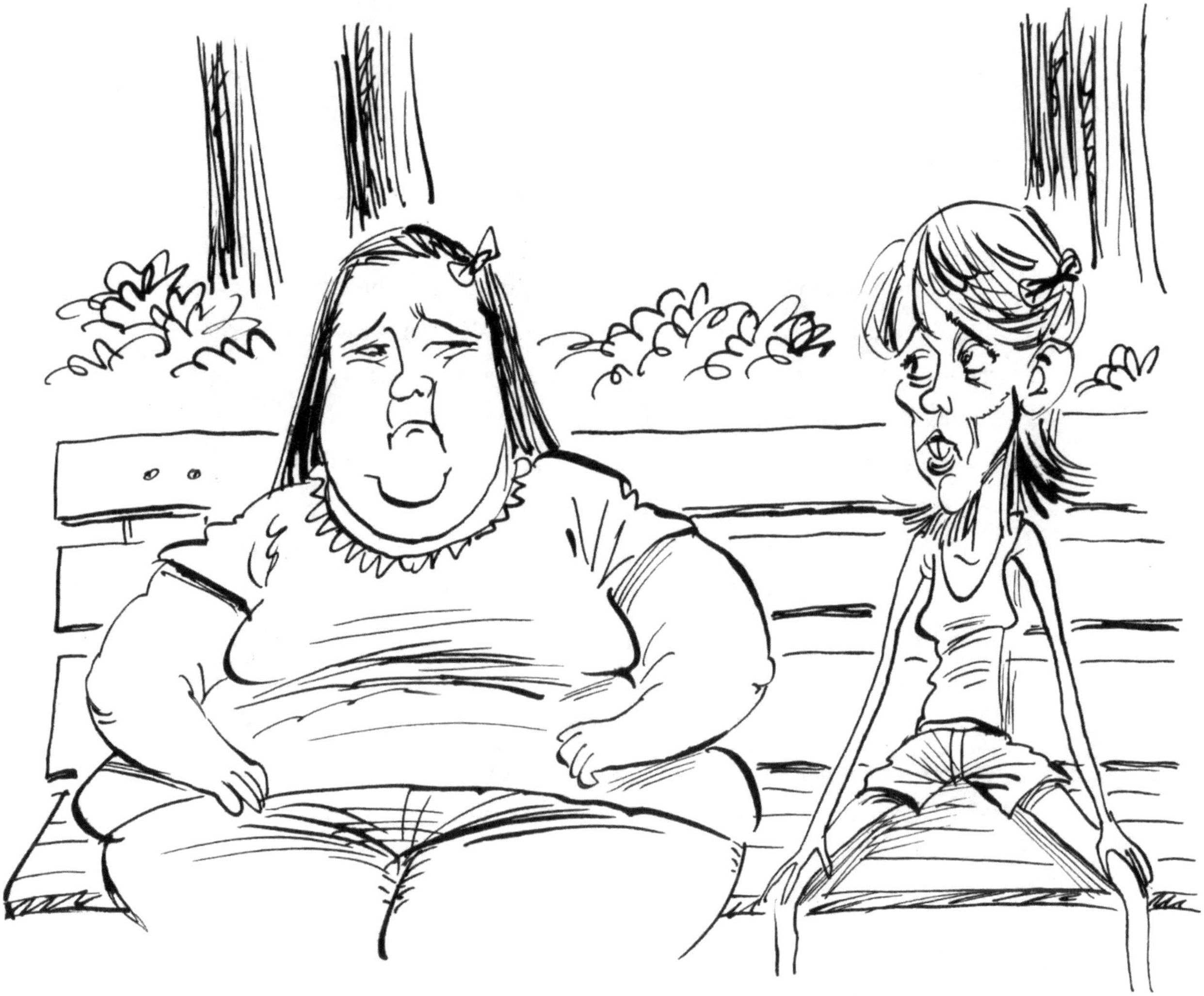

DIET AND NUTRITION

It is often said, "We are what we eat." There is no question that this statement is true, but we must also accept that there is a large genetic component, inherited from our parents, that has already been programmed into our bodies. Our social environment and activity levels also play a huge role.

In much earlier times, food was scarce. Humans devoted their lives to finding or cultivating what they needed. Mankind has progressed over the years, but in that evolution, food has become, for many, too plentiful and easily available. For a large number of people, this has led to obesity. For others, there is a great deal of emphasis on beauty, physical fitness, and thinness in their lives. Each extreme can have devastating effects for both women and men. The perception that each of us can have a perfect body is, for the vast majority, unrealistic and unattainable.

Some knowledge is necessary to understand our food requirements. A balanced diet consists of six main components. Carbohydrates, such as sugar, starch, and fibres (bread etc.) are our only source for cellular energy. Fats (butter etc.), known as lipids, are an important component of each cell, because they store energy and essential nutrients. Proteins (meat), made up of amino acids, are the building blocks for our bodies. Minerals (calcium, iron, magnesium, sodium, etc.) and vitamins (D, C, A etc.), which are micronutrients, are required in trace amounts for cellular activity. Also, because our bodies consist mainly of water, adequate fluid intake is essential.

TEENAGE OBESITY

If people weigh 20% or more than doctors consider normal for their height, they are considered fat or obese. Obesity, which has increased substantially over the last few decades, is now considered a health epidemic. Over 30% of children and teenagers in North America are considered overweight. Obese children and teenagers often remain significantly overweight into adulthood. Being overweight puts stress on the joints and affects not only breathing and sleep, but mood and energy levels as well. Ultimately, being overweight can lead to heart disease, increased blood pressure, diabetes, and strokes. Psychologically, there is loss of self-esteem, often resulting in depression.

The many causes of obesity are often interrelated. Certainly genetics can play a role, but over-eating is also cultural in an obese family. For some people, food is comforting; it makes them happy. Many families have unhealthy diets that include poor food choices, namely excessive carbohydrate intake (junk foods, such as potato chips, cookies, pasta, sugary drinks). Because these foods are the cheapest, families on a limited budget often have fewer healthy options that they can afford.

Lifestyle Choices

Education is necessary if our obese culture is to be changed. A balanced diet of vegetables, fruits, whole grain cereals, and protein is important, with decreased consumption of carbohydrates, sugars, and fats. For many of us food is readily available, affordable, and enjoyable. Snacking between meals is common, but it can result in the overconsumption of calories and a slow but steady increase in weight.

Discipline and portion control are essential to maintaining a normal body weight. Fortunately, exercise helps burn off excessive caloric intake. If you eat more calories than you use, these additional calories, usually from sugar, are turned into fat and stored. Since food is fuel, you shouldn't eat more than necessary to maintain an ideal body weight.

ANOREXIA

In advertisements, magazines, movies, television, and on the Internet, we are bombarded with images of thin, beautiful, women and muscular, handsome men. This false portrayal of "normality" has resulted in an industry catering to beauty, fitness, and dieting. There is nothing wrong with eating better, exercising, and taking care of yourself and your appearance. But for many, especially young teenage women, there is a fine line between watching your weight and cultivating an eating disorder. With our own unique genetic make-ups, we are all not pre-programmed to be thin or have handsome features. Striving to obtain the perfect body can become compulsive and self-destructive. Concern over weight and body image can affect every part of the person's life: their thoughts, feelings, and relationships. In some young people, the desire for thinness causes severe health problems and can potentially be fatal.

Teenage years can be troubling, especially for maturing young girls. Because there are social pressures to look a certain way, young girls may be frightened and concerned by their body changes during puberty. Cultural pressure also exists to look like and be someone other than who you truly are.

About one in a hundred teenage girls develops a condition called anorexia nervosa. First, the young girl cuts down the portions she eats or misses meals in an attempt to lose weight. Over time, she becomes more focused on this endeavour, until soon her weight is all she thinks about. The teen may turn to excessive exercise in the hope that it will make her body perfect. When diet and exercise fail to change her self-perception, she begins to routinely skip meals, fast, and refuse to eat with others. She becomes a calorie counter, often weighing and measuring her food. Still not satisfied, she can turn to even more radical options.

BULIMIA

Bulimia refers to the condition wherein individuals purges themselves of food by inducing vomiting, taking a laxative, or using diuretics in an attempt to remove calories or weight from their body. We can see this in "binge eaters" or in the advanced stages of anorexia. This extreme behaviour can be observed early on or later in individuals with eating disorders. Needless to say, purging can have very severe consequences.

Once excessive dieting or purging becomes an issue, certain things happen in and to the body of the teenager. Because food is our source of energy, when there are fewer calories available to us, we will often notice poor concentration, memory loss, irritability, mood swings, anxiety, and depression. The teenager feels cold all the time, may lose her hair, and periods often become irregular and may stop altogether. In addition, the heart rate slows, accompanied by low blood pressure. Bones become thin and fragile, growth can be stunted, and tooth enamel breaks down. If bulimia is prolonged, and both medical and psychological interventions prove unhelpful, those with a severe disorder can and do die from starvation.

EXERCISE

Regular exercise is important for all of us, but particularly for young children, adolescents, and teenagers. Experts believe that at least sixty minutes a day of moderate to vigorous activity is ideal. Exercise not only controls weight by burning up calories, but also increases strength and muscle mass, which protects joints from injury, while boosting energy levels. There are also less obvious but important long-term positive effects: a decrease in blood pressure, a decrease in heart rate, an increase in bone mass, and a lesser incidence of diabetes.

Emotionally, exercise improves mood and lessens the likelihood of depression. Being physically tired after exercise leads to better sleep patterns. Feeling good increases one's self-esteem and outwardly enhances self-confidence. Thinking and learning skills improve.

Nearly all forms of exercise are helpful. Routine walking, running, hiking, swimming, and biking are all easy and readily available. Strength training, from push-ups to leg raises to more specific muscle-strengthening exercises, requires more dedication. Joining a gym can be very positive, but is usually unnecessary to stay healthy.

After childhood, many teenagers become less active physically. Increasing school demands and an emerging social life hamper getting out and about. Distractions, especially the Internet—a very sedentary pastime—are more prevalent and detract from a healthy physical lifestyle. Undoubtedly, hours of sitting can and will lead to health consequences, physically, mentally, and emotionally.

Chapter Fifteen

INTERNET AND THE TEENAGE DRIVER

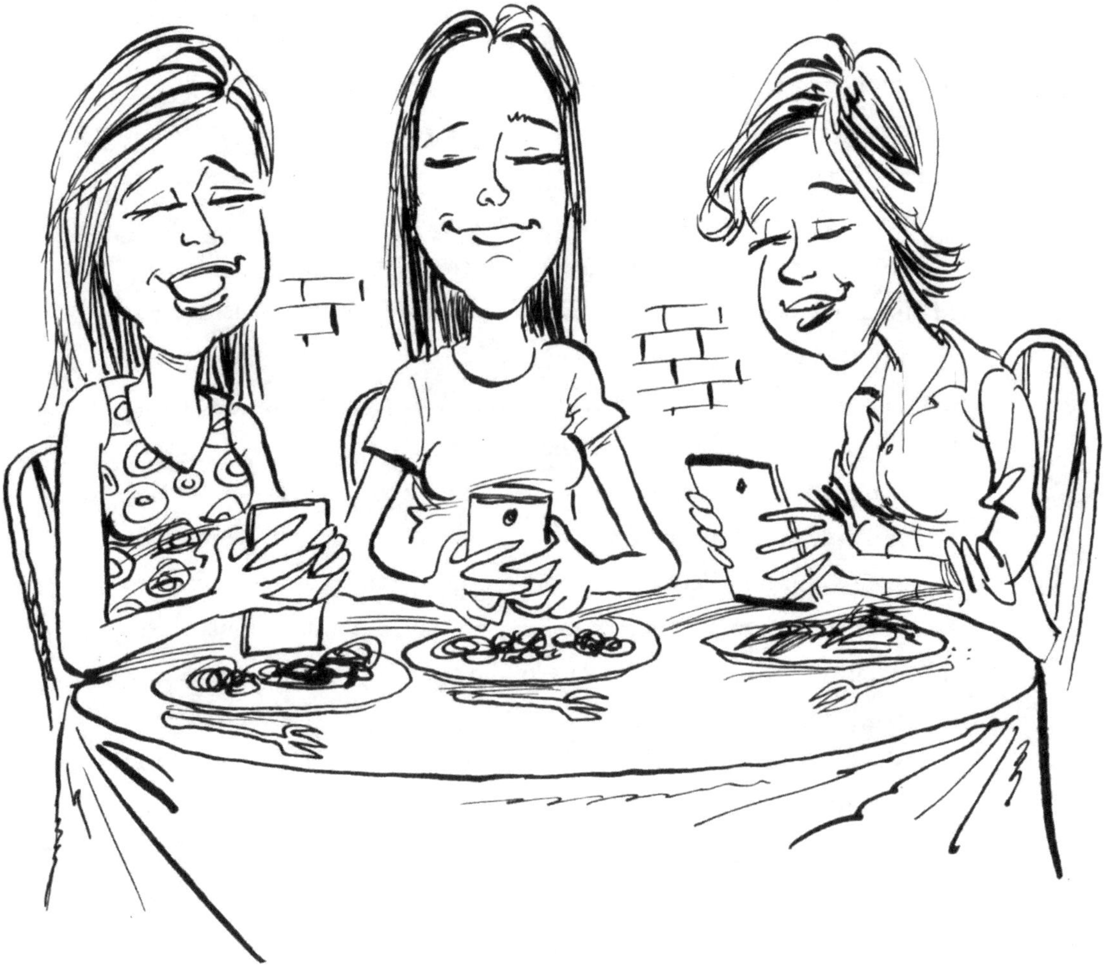

THE INTERNET, SOCIAL MEDIA, AND GAMING

Computers, and especially the Internet, have transformed all of us in both the developed and emerging worlds. Teenagers have probably been affected the most. Not only do they get the majority of their information from the Internet, they also have an extremely large presence on social media and gaming sites. Text messaging on mobile phones seems to be the most popular method of communication.

The Internet, having made access to information readily available, has enhanced the teenager's understanding of the wider world. If it is used properly, this young generation will have greater academic opportunities than their parents. So much material is readily available without spending countless hours in the library. Reviewing large amounts of data from different sites can enhance the adolescent's abilities to interpret and integrate information. Other benefits include improving one's writing and thinking skills. However, not all the information found on the Internet is accurate or worth looking at, so young minds must learn to sort out what is valuable by developing their critical thinking skills. This takes time.

If the Internet is used excessively (for hours a day) or inappropriately (by aimlessly looking and playing around), it can become a real problem. Overuse of the Internet has become like a drug and may over time, if not curtailed, become addictive. Too often young people bounce from site to site, exploring whatever. Disturbing content, viewed by "accident", can leave a deep and lasting impression. There is usually no control over what they can see. It has become a place to "hang out".

There are many social media sites (Facebook, Twitter, Instagram, Snapchat, etc.) where the young chat; it gives them an opportunity to connect with others. Girls are more inclined than boys to use social media to communicate. These sites can be a healthy and efficient way to stay connected. In other circumstances, they provide anonymity for those who wish to promote alternate identities. By being online, teens can grow isolated, drawing inward into their Internet world. Direct face-to-face communication skills may be lost. Being able to hold a meaningful in-person conversation is a skill desperately needed for success later in life, i.e. for higher education and for entry into the job market.

The risks of social networking are many. Bullying and harassment are of great concern. Messages can be demeaning, often indecent or racist, and may even incite violence. The young teenager may be contacted anonymously or by an adult predator. Needless to say, the teen can be completely overwhelmed by the situation. Without taking great care, the teenager can be victimized if his or her personal information is disclosed. In addition there are financial risks if credit card or banking information is released unknowingly.

There are literally thousands of online games that consume many teenagers' time. Young men seem to be most susceptible, and once they are "hooked", it becomes an obsession. Gaming detracts from normal activities such as school, athletics, social interaction, and work opportunities.

Like it or not, the increased presence of the young online is a reality. However, too much screen-time certainly has negative consequences. Naturally, there are serious concerns regarding the content and safety of social media sites. It is difficult for a teenager to self-regulate, as there is a lack of insight into any harmful effects certain sites may have. Beyond the normal concerns of wasting time that could be better spent, there is always a concern about gossip, name-calling, threats, and cyber bullying. Sexual exploitation is well documented; too often young girls, for whatever reason, carelessly expose themselves, either by sexting or posting nude photos online. Once online, the information is there for a very long time. Years later, foolish comments or photos can reappear. Tragically, some teenagers have been so disturbed by what they have done that suicide seems like the only way to save face. *Potential employers, years later, will search for your presence on Internet sites. If something negative is found you may be out of luck for employment. Not something you would want!*

WHEELS: RISKS AND CONCERNS

From being a toddler to one's teenage years, there is a fascination for being on wheels. It is not long after learning to walk and get around that you are given a toy with wheels. You climb aboard and soon learn how fun it is to move faster and further with little effort. Next you learn to ride a tricycle and then a bicycle with training wheels. The ultimate freedom happens when those support wheels are removed and you are on your own and off to further explore your neighbourhood. Before long, you become brave enough to venture off your own street. Then, as you get older and more confident, you become able get about town.

Learning to ride a bike is challenging at first, with many bumps and bruises to show for the effort. Fortunately, by using your own power, you can't go too fast. But you must learn how to ride safely, respect others on the road, and negotiate traffic on busy roads. Even when one is taking proper care on a bicycle, severe injuries can take place.

Once you reach a certain age, usually sixteen to eighteen (but in some areas as late as twenty-one), you are permitted to learn how to drive a motor vehicle and get a license, providing you have passed the qualifying examination. In different jurisdictions there may be different requirements for independent driving. The reason for this is that there is no universal agreement about when young people are mature enough or experienced enough to take the wheel and go anywhere they want on their own. It is hard for a new driver to appreciate all the issues and risks associated with driving a motor vehicle in every situation, i.e. heavy traffic, rain, night-time, snow, blinding lights, etc.

Many teenagers think they are invincible and know everything. This, of course, is far from the truth and becomes most obvious with respect to new drivers.

SOME STARTLING FACTS

1) The risk for motor vehicle accidents is higher amongst sixteen to nineteen-year-olds than any other age group.

2) Drivers between the ages of sixteen and nineteen are three times more likely than those aged twenty or older to be involved in a fatal crash.

RISK FACTORS

1) Lack of experience and skill. Teenagers often underestimate dangerous situations.

2) Teenagers are more likely to speed. There can be a tendency to show off and become reckless.

3) They may drive aggressively.

4) They have the lowest rate of seatbelt use.

5) Other teenagers in the car often cause distractions.

6) Male drivers are more at risk than female drivers. Two out of every three teenagers killed are males.

7) Teenagers sometimes drive under the influence of alcohol or marijuana.

8) They may use a cell phone or text while driving.

9) They are often distracted while driving, by music, cell phones or people on the street

10) Friday, Saturday, and Sunday, when teens are most often driving, have the highest accident rates.

When the key for a car or truck is first handed over to a teenager, lives are at risk, and there is potential for car and property damage. Never before has the teenager been in control (or out of control) of something as powerful as a car. Any vehicle inherently has the capacity to severely injure or kill them or others. That is why, in some areas, "graduated licenses" are becoming more popular. A graduated license allows the novice driver to gain driving experience with supervision. An inexperienced driver can't drive at night or alone, or with only other teenagers in the car, etc. Others can identify the car that the newly licensed driver is using, as it is marked by an "N" or "L" or other such symbol.

Learning to drive and gaining the proper skills to minimize accidents require years of experience. Driving is a real responsibility, not only to yourself, but also to your passengers, other cars, motorcyclists, bicyclists, and pedestrians on the road. A serious accident can and often does have lifelong consequences for all involved.

Never ever drink or use drugs while driving. As a passenger, never get into the car with a driver who has been drinking or using drugs, or any car in which you feel unsafe. There is always another way home. Most importantly, SPEED KILLS! *Your life is too precious!*

Chapter Sixteen

BECOMING AN ADULT

Eighteen-Plus

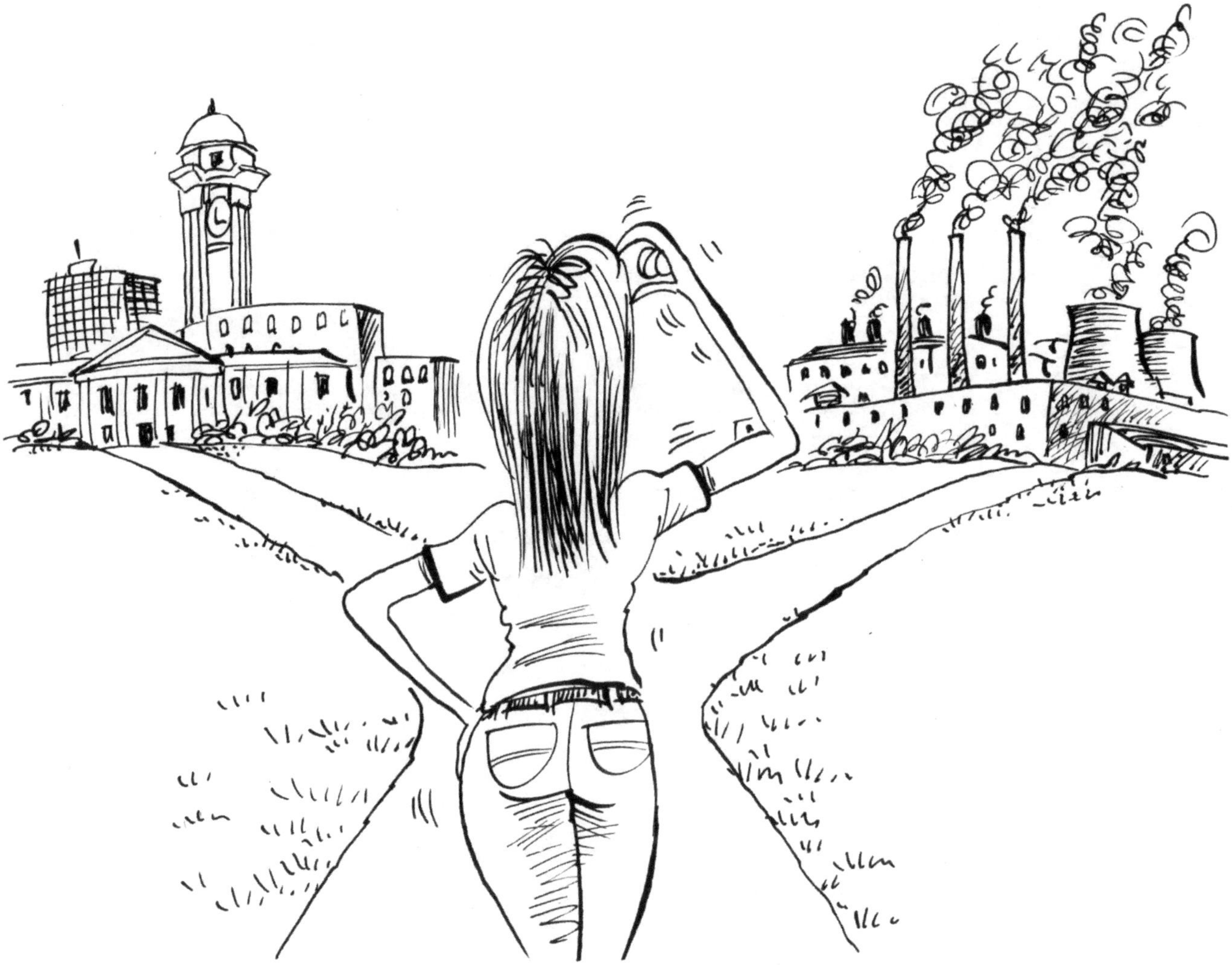

Becoming an Adult

After your eighteenth birthday you are considered an adult, with all the freedoms and benefits that this entails. However, you're not finished growing, intellectually, emotionally, or spiritually. That will take a lifetime. Initially, you will face new challenges and responsibilities as you set your sails on your own course through adulthood and on life's adventure.

HIGHER EDUCATION

At this point in your life's journey you must decide whether to continue your formal education. Wisely, most young adults recognize that more training would be beneficial, and they decide either to learn a skill or to go on to university, with the years and financial commitment that this involves. If you choose to follow an academic career, do you or your family have the resources required, or are you prepared to take out a student loan to pursue higher education? A university degree can have many career benefits and enrich you both personally and professionally over the long term. However, you may or may not have the aptitude or desire for continued "book learning" and might prefer to pursue more practical education to provide the resources necessary to support yourself throughout your life. You choose.

For most parents, there is a timeline regarding their willingness to fully support their children financially. From an educational, emotional, and financial perspective, parents too are looking forward to your independence. You are becoming fully aware of the tremendous costs associated with living independently. It is not cheap to feed, clothe, and house yourself, and that responsibility becomes increasingly front and center as you look down the road.

Even though the prospect looks daunting, each of us needs to embrace the opportunity to be totally in charge of our own destiny. In today's sophisticated world, once we complete our formal education, we look for a job, start to work, and usually, during this time frame, find a permanent partner, a husband or wife, and consider whether to have our own children.

FINAL THOUGHTS

There is a natural rhythm and cycle to our lives. From birth to death, there is a certain sameness to the human experience for all races and cultures. After birth, if we are to be truly fulfilled, we all require protection, food, and clothing, as well as emotional bonds with our parents, family, society, and our own culture. We must all learn not only a language, but also all sorts of information and skills in order to survive and prosper. Most importantly, we must learn to respect others, no matter their education, background, wealth, religion, colour of their skin, or culture. None of us is perfect, or ever will be. We all have strengths and weaknesses; the cumulative result of our life experiences. Our character, moulded over the years, is difficult to change, but we must all work on our deficiencies and try always to be better people.

Strive to have balance between work and play in your life, while making time for others. Remember, though, that you need time for yourself and your own private reflections. Enjoy each day as if it were your last.

No other person is like you. Embrace your situation. Hopefully, you are in a position to thank your parents, family, schools, and culture for who you are. It is on their shoulders you stand. They gave you both

"ROOTS AND WINGS"
…go fly!

Take care of yourself, of course, but remember… what really matters in life is:
WHAT YOU DO FOR OTHERS.

ACKNOWLEDGEMENTS

First and foremost, I want to thank my wife Liz for not only supporting my compulsive desire to write this book, but to become its first critic and editor. Medical doctors are universally known to have poor handwriting (this was written in longhand), but are not necessarily the best English scholars either. I have written many medical articles in the past, but a book attempting to appeal to ten to eighteen-year olds was new to me. As young people in this age group have very little life experience or scientific background, I tried to simplify things as best I could, yet address the issues head-on.

My wonderful wife of over fifty years typed the manuscript, provided useful insight and made it presentable, hopefully readable and engaging for its first draft. Needless to say, she found some of the topics difficult, but recognized the truth that life's early challenges had to be presented if they were to be avoided. Without her support, wisdom and constant attention to detail, you would not be reading this book.

Second, it was always my intention to try to present some difficult subject matter with a touch of humour through illustrations (never an easy combination). Searching the Internet, I was directed to Ian Baker in the United Kingdom, half a world away. Ian is a true professional artist, with more than twenty years of experience in illustrating and writing. Surprisingly, he agreed to work with me to try to capture the essence of the text through cartoon-like drawings, but he was also able to interpret and simplify the scientific and medical aspects surrounding human growth. He did a superb job; my thanks go out to him. For, without his talents, this book would not have been nearly as interesting or enjoyable. A picture does speak a thousand words.

Next, I wish to thank our three children, Robin, Christie and Drew, for giving me the inspiration to pass along what I have learned as their father to our grandchildren. The greatest privilege in life is to be a parent, with an opportunity to shape the lives of the next generation. Our children and grandchildren are the delight of my life; nothing else really matters.

Fourth, I extend my gratitude to all my patients, young and old, for trusting and having confidence in me. I had the privilege of caring for thousands of patients over the years, from every culture and walk of life. It mattered not whether they were rich or poor, educated or not – they all provided me with insight into their life struggles.

Last, I must thank our publisher, FriesenPress, who supported my idea to reach out to a wider audience, as they believed in the project. I had no idea a whole team would become involved, all with different skills, to make the book a reality. My initial desire was only to help our grandchildren with the inevitable stresses of their early lives. However, friends and colleagues encouraged me to reach out to other youngsters and their families, in the hope that more young people would benefit and avoid at least some pain. If I am able to keep one person from the "hard to do" issues, especially those that end in long term health problems or death, I will find my efforts rewarded.

Nanoose Bay, British Columbia
September 2017

ABOUT THE AUTHOR

J.E.H. Spence, MD, FRCS(C) received his medical degree from the University of Western Ontario, Canada. After two years of internship, travel, and general practice, he specialized in obstetrics and gynecology. Having developed a particular interest in the medical issues of young females, he moved to London, England and studied under Professor Sir John Dewhurst at the Chelsea Hospital for Women and Great Ormond Street Children's Hospital. After returning to Canada, Dr. Spence headed up the Division of Pediatric and Adolescent Gynecology at the Children's Hospital of Eastern Ontario. He became Chief of the Division of Reproductive Medicine, Chief of Obstetrics and Gynecology at the Ottawa Civic Hospital, and Professor of Obstetrics and Gynecology at the University of Ottawa. He has lectured throughout North America and abroad and has published numerous articles on his areas of interest. Dr. Spence is now retired and dedicates his time to volunteer work. He and his wife of fifty years now live on beautiful Vancouver Island, British Columbia.

ABOUT THE ILLUSTRATOR

Ian Baker has been one of the United Kingdom's leading cartoonists, illustrators and comedy writers for over twenty years. His work has been featured in many of the world's most prestigious publications (*The Times, The Independent on Sunday, The Spectator, The New Statesman, Punch, Penthouse* and many others). He has illustrated dozens of books, as well as writing his own. Ian has also worked in television, writing for various comedy series, His advertising work has included commissions for a multitude of corporate international giants. He lives and works in Sheffield, England.

Printed in Canada